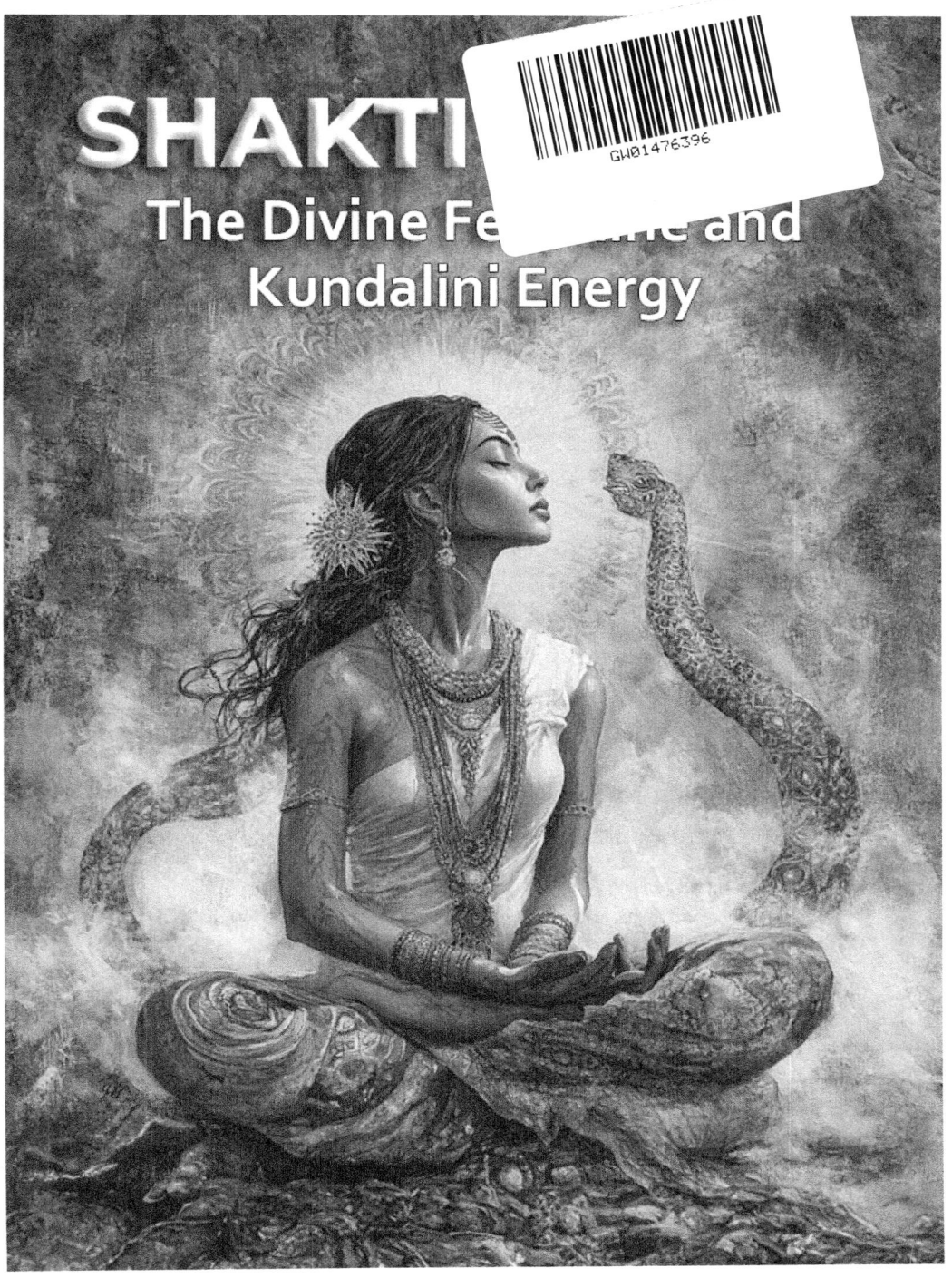

SHAKTI
The Divine Feminine and Kundalini Energy

Part I: The Essence of Shakti

The Awakening of Shakti: Understanding the Divine Feminine as the Source of All Creation

Shakti is the primordial, divine feminine energy that permeates the universe. It is the creative force behind all existence, the dynamic power that moves and animates life. In many spiritual traditions, especially in Hinduism and Tantra, Shakti is seen as both the cosmic principle of energy and an intimately personal force within each being. Awakening Shakti is the process of realizing, embodying, and channeling this immense power, leading to transformation, spiritual evolution, and enlightenment.

---

1. What is Shakti?

Shakti is a Sanskrit word meaning "power" or "energy." It represents the feminine aspect of the divine, which is not separate from the masculine (Shiva) but exists in a dynamic interplay with it. If Shiva is consciousness, Shakti is the force that brings consciousness into action. She is the life-giving, nurturing, and transformative energy that sustains the cosmos.

In Hindu mythology, Shakti is often personified as goddesses such as:

- **Parvati** – The nurturing and loving aspect of Shakti.
- **Durga** – The fierce protector and warrior goddess.
- **Kali** – The force of destruction and renewal.
- **Lakshmi** – The goddess of abundance and prosperity.
- **Saraswati** – The embodiment of wisdom and creativity.

These deities are not just symbolic; they represent different facets of Shakti that exist within every individual.

---

2. Shakti as the Source of All Creation

The Cosmic Dance of Creation

According to Hindu cosmology, the universe is born out of the dance between Shiva and Shakti. While Shiva represents stillness, Shakti is the movement that brings everything into existence. This divine interplay mirrors the fundamental principles of creation—matter and energy, consciousness and dynamism, potential and manifestation.

In the **Devi Bhagavata Purana**, Shakti is described as the **Adi Shakti**, the original power from which everything emerges. The universe is not seen as created by an external god but as a manifestation of Shakti's own will and play (Lila).

Manifestation at the Micro and Macro Levels

- **At the Macro Level** – Shakti is the energy that sustains the planets, the stars, the elements, and all life forms. She is present in the natural world, the cycles of life and death, and the forces of destruction and renewal.
- **At the Micro Level** – Shakti exists within every being as **Kundalini energy**, the dormant spiritual force coiled at the base of the spine. When awakened, this energy rises through the chakras, leading to spiritual transformation and self-realization.

---

3. The Awakening of Shakti in the Individual

How Does Shakti Remain Dormant?

Most people live in a state where Shakti is dormant or only partially awakened. This can be due to conditioning, fear, trauma, or an overemphasis on logic and intellect (masculine energy). Without awakening, life may feel stagnant, uninspired, or disconnected from its full potential.

What Does Awakening Shakti Feel Like?

When Shakti begins to awaken, it is often experienced as:

- A surge of **energy** and vitality.
- A deep sense of **intuition** and inner knowing.
- Heightened **creativity** and inspiration.
- Intense emotional releases and healing.
- A longing for **spiritual connection** and purpose.

Ways to Awaken Shakti

1. **Meditation on the Divine Feminine** – Focusing on goddess archetypes or chanting Devi mantras like **Om Shakti Namaha** or **Om Dum Durgayei Namaha**.
2. **Pranayama (Breathwork)** – Activating life force energy through breath control.
3. **Yoga** – Especially Kundalini Yoga and practices that emphasize movement, flow, and energy activation.
4. **Dance and Sacred Movement** – Expressing Shakti through the body, especially in forms like belly dancing, Odissi, or ecstatic dance.
5. **Connection to Nature** – Spending time in natural spaces where Shakti's presence is strong—forests, rivers, mountains.

6. **Tantric Practices** – Working with sacred sexuality and energy activation to merge with Shakti's power.
7. **Shadow Work** – Healing repressed emotions, traumas, and fears that block the flow of Shakti.

4. Shakti in Everyday Life

Awakening Shakti is not just about mystical experiences—it is about living in alignment with divine feminine energy in daily life. When Shakti is awakened, a person becomes more:

- **Authentic** – Living in truth, passion, and creative expression.
- **Empowered** – No longer afraid to step into their power and potential.
- **Compassionate** – Embodying the nurturing and healing aspects of the Divine Feminine.
- **Courageous** – Fearlessly embracing change and transformation, much like the warrior goddess Durga.

Women and men alike can benefit from Shakti's awakening, as it brings balance to both **masculine and feminine energies** within. In a world dominated by action, control, and logic, reclaiming Shakti is a return to intuition, flow, and sacred wisdom.

5. The Global Rise of Shakti

In recent times, we are witnessing a collective awakening of Shakti energy worldwide. The resurgence of interest in spirituality, feminine wisdom, and holistic healing is a sign of this shift. Movements advocating for environmental consciousness, women's empowerment, and community healing are all reflections of Shakti rising at a global level.

This is not just a personal transformation—it is a cosmic unfolding. As more people awaken to Shakti, a new era of balance, harmony, and higher consciousness emerges.

The journey of awakening Shakti is the journey of returning to our most **authentic, powerful, and creative selves**. She is the fire in our soul, the rhythm in our heartbeat, and the wisdom in our intuition. To awaken Shakti is to awaken life itself.

Whether through meditation, movement, nature, or devotion, every step taken towards Shakti is a step toward **wholeness, transformation, and divine realization**.

For our free video kundalini training visit https://shiftnetwork.infusionsoft.com/go/akeg/a20331

The Sacred Energy Within – What is Kundalini, and Why is it Vital to Spiritual Evolution?

Kundalini is the **latent spiritual energy** that resides within every human being, waiting to be awakened. Often described as a **coiled serpent** at the base of the spine, this energy represents the raw, divine potential within us—the life force that fuels spiritual awakening, higher consciousness, and self-realization.

The process of awakening Kundalini has been explored for thousands of years in mystical traditions, particularly in **Tantra, Yoga, and Vedanta**, as well as other esoteric spiritual systems around the world. When activated, Kundalini moves through the body's **subtle energy system**, opening the chakras and leading to profound personal transformation.

This chapter delves into what Kundalini is, how it functions, and why it plays a crucial role in **spiritual evolution and self-discovery**.

---

1. What is Kundalini Energy?

The Meaning of Kundalini

The word **Kundalini** comes from the Sanskrit root *kundal*, meaning **coiled** or **circular**. In ancient texts, it is depicted as a **serpent** curled three and a half times at the base of the spine, lying dormant in the **Muladhara (Root) Chakra** until it is awakened.

Kundalini is also known as:

- **Shakti Energy** – The divine feminine power within.
- **Serpent Power** – The symbol of transformation and spiritual potential.
- **Life Force Energy** – The vital energy that sustains consciousness and existence.

It is the **source of all energy, wisdom, and creativity** within us. However, in most people, it remains **dormant**, influencing life only in subtle ways. The goal of spiritual evolution is to **awaken Kundalini**, allowing it to rise through the chakras, leading to enlightenment (*Samadhi*).

---

2. The Subtle Body: How Kundalini Moves

The Three Energy Channels (Nadis)

Kundalini does not move through the **physical body** but rather through the **subtle body**, composed of **energy channels (nadis) and chakras**. The three main nadis are:

1. **Ida Nadi** (Left Channel) – Represents the **moon, feminine energy, intuition, and emotions**. It governs the left side of the body.

For our free chakra energy training course visit https://chakra.gr8.com/

2. **Pingala Nadi** (Right Channel) – Represents the **sun, masculine energy, logic, and action**. It governs the right side of the body.
3. **Sushumna Nadi** (Central Channel) – The **main energy pathway**, running along the spine. Kundalini rises through this channel when activated.

When Kundalini is dormant, **Ida and Pingala** control our physical and mental states. But when Kundalini awakens, it ascends through **Sushumna Nadi**, piercing the **seven chakras**, leading to expanded awareness and enlightenment.

The Seven Chakras and Kundalini Awakening

As Kundalini ascends, it activates the **seven chakras**, which represent different levels of consciousness:

1. **Muladhara (Root Chakra)** – Grounding, survival, basic instincts.
2. **Swadhisthana (Sacral Chakra)** – Emotions, creativity, sexuality.
3. **Manipura (Solar Plexus Chakra)** – Power, confidence, self-identity.
4. **Anahata (Heart Chakra)** – Love, compassion, connection.
5. **Vishuddha (Throat Chakra)** – Expression, truth, communication.
6. **Ajna (Third Eye Chakra)** – Intuition, wisdom, inner vision.
7. **Sahasrara (Crown Chakra)** – Enlightenment, divine consciousness.

The full awakening of Kundalini results in **spiritual enlightenment**, or **Samadhi**, where the individual consciousness merges with the divine.

---

3. Why is Kundalini Vital to Spiritual Evolution?

Kundalini is not just a mystical energy—it is the **driving force behind personal and spiritual evolution**. Here's why it is essential:

1. Unlocking Higher States of Consciousness

When Kundalini awakens, it **shifts perception** beyond the ordinary mind, leading to **expanded awareness, intuition, and divine realization**. It dissolves the illusion of separation, allowing one to experience **oneness with the universe**.

2. Awakening Dormant Potential

Kundalini enhances **mental clarity, creativity, and intelligence**. Many great artists, scientists, and spiritual leaders unknowingly tap into this energy when experiencing moments of inspiration or deep insight.

3. Purification and Healing

As Kundalini rises, it **burns away karma, past traumas, and emotional blockages**, leading to deep healing and personal transformation. This process, while intense, is necessary for spiritual evolution.

4. Activating Intuition and Psychic Abilities

An awakened Kundalini enhances **intuition, clairvoyance, telepathy, and spiritual sensitivity**, making it easier to perceive higher dimensions of reality.

5. Aligning with Divine Purpose

When Kundalini is awakened, individuals feel a **sense of divine purpose**. Life becomes deeply meaningful, and one naturally aligns with their **soul's mission**.

---

4. The Kundalini Awakening Process

Kundalini awakening can occur in different ways:

1. Spontaneous Awakening

- Can happen after a deep spiritual experience, near-death experience, or trauma.
- May be sudden and overwhelming.

2. Gradual Awakening

- Develops through meditation, breathwork, yoga, and spiritual practices.
- More stable and easier to integrate into daily life.

3. Transmission from a Guru (Shaktipat)

- Some receive direct energy activation from a **spiritual master**.
- Can be instantaneous but requires preparation to handle the energy.

---

5. The Challenges of Kundalini Awakening

While Kundalini awakening is a profound journey, it can also be challenging. Some common difficulties include:

- **Physical Symptoms** – Heat sensations, spontaneous body movements, headaches.
- **Emotional Upheavals** – Deep fears, past trauma surfacing, mood swings.
- **Ego Dissolution** – Loss of identity, confusion, existential questioning.

- **Disconnection from Society** – Feeling alienated or struggling to relate to others.

Proper guidance, **self-care, and grounding practices** are essential to navigate these challenges.

6. How to Prepare for Kundalini Awakening

If approached consciously, Kundalini awakening can be a **beautiful, life-changing experience**. Here are ways to **prepare**:

1. **Meditation and Mindfulness** – Calms the mind and prepares it for higher consciousness.
2. **Pranayama (Breathwork)** – Balances energy flow and prepares the nervous system.
3. **Yoga** – Especially **Kundalini Yoga, Hatha Yoga**, and **Tantric practices**.
4. **Mantra Chanting** – Sacred sounds like "**Om Namah Shivaya**" or "**Sat Nam**" activate Kundalini.
5. **Self-Inquiry and Shadow Work** – Healing inner wounds to allow energy to flow freely.
6. **Living with Awareness** – Cultivating love, gratitude, and mindfulness in daily life.

Shakti in Ancient Traditions – Hinduism, Tantra, and Global Representations of the Divine Feminine

The concept of **Shakti, the Divine Feminine energy**, is one of the most ancient and universal spiritual principles found across cultures and traditions. It represents the **creative, sustaining, and transformative power** of the universe—both at the cosmic level and within each individual. In various traditions, Shakti takes on different names and forms, yet the essence remains the same: **She is the source of life, wisdom, and evolution.**

This chapter explores Shakti in Hinduism, Tantra, and other global traditions that honor the Divine Feminine.

1. Shakti in Hinduism: The Supreme Creative Force

In **Hinduism**, Shakti is not just an abstract energy but is worshiped as **the supreme goddess**, embodying all aspects of creation, preservation, and destruction. Unlike many Western traditions that place divinity solely in masculine form, Hinduism recognizes that divine energy must be both **masculine (Shiva) and feminine (Shakti)** for the universe to function.

The Three Major Aspects of Shakti

Shakti expresses herself in different forms, each representing a particular **power (Shakti)**:

1. **Saraswati (Wisdom and Creativity Shakti)**
   - Goddess of knowledge, music, and art.
   - Associated with the **flow of inspiration, speech, and learning**.
   - Symbolizes the **intellectual and creative force** necessary for civilization to thrive.

2. **Lakshmi (Prosperity and Abundance Shakti)**
   - Goddess of wealth, beauty, and fertility.
   - Brings **material and spiritual prosperity**.
   - Represents **balance, harmony, and the nourishment of life**.

3. **Kali/Durga (Power and Transformation Shakti)**
   - Fierce warrior goddess who destroys **evil and ignorance**.
   - Kali is the **dark, primal aspect of Shakti**, dissolving the ego to bring enlightenment.
   - Durga rides a lion or tiger, symbolizing her **unconquerable strength**.

These forms are not separate entities; they are different **expressions of the same cosmic force**, appearing as needed.

Shakti and Shiva: The Divine Union

Shakti is often depicted alongside **Shiva**, the masculine principle of pure consciousness. Their relationship is **symbolic of the cosmic balance**:

- **Shiva without Shakti is inactive and unmanifest.**
- **Shakti without Shiva is directionless and chaotic.**
- **Together, they create, sustain, and dissolve reality.**

This dynamic interplay is represented in **Tantric philosophy** as **Ardhanarishvara**, the half-male, half-female form of Shiva-Shakti, demonstrating their **inseparability**.

---

2. Shakti in Tantra: The Path of Divine Feminine Power

What is Tantra?

Tantra is a **spiritual tradition** that deeply reveres Shakti, considering her the **path to liberation** (*moksha*). Unlike ascetic traditions that renounce the physical world, Tantra sees **all of life—including the body, emotions, and desires—as sacred expressions of Shakti**.

Kundalini Shakti: The Inner Awakening

In Tantra, the **most powerful form of Shakti** is known as **Kundalini**, the dormant serpent energy coiled at the base of the spine. Through specific **practices like yoga, breathwork, and mantra chanting**, Kundalini can be awakened, leading to:

- Higher states of consciousness.
- Deep inner transformation.
- Union with divine awareness.

The ultimate goal of Tantra is to **unite Kundalini Shakti (dynamic energy) with Shiva (pure consciousness), leading to enlightenment.**

Sacred Sexuality and Tantric Rituals

Tantra also embraces **sacred sexuality** as a means to awaken divine energy. Unlike conventional perspectives on sexuality, Tantra sees it as a **spiritual gateway**—a way to experience **oneness with the universe**.

However, Tantra is **not just about sexuality**—it is a **holistic spiritual path** that incorporates meditation, devotion, and rituals to **honor the Divine Feminine in all aspects of life**.

---

3. Shakti in Global Traditions: The Universal Goddess

The reverence for the **Divine Feminine** is not unique to Hinduism or Tantra; it is a **universal theme** found in ancient cultures worldwide. Many civilizations have worshiped powerful **goddesses** who embody the same forces as Shakti.

1. Egypt: Isis – The Goddess of Magic and Motherhood

- **Isis** was the **mother goddess**, protector of the dead, and the **embodiment of divine wisdom**.
- She was seen as the **source of creation, healing, and transformation**—much like **Shakti in Hinduism**.
- **Her worship spread beyond Egypt**, influencing later traditions in Greece and Rome.

2. Greece & Rome: Aphrodite/Venus and Athena/Minerva

- **Aphrodite (Venus)** – Goddess of love, beauty, and fertility, similar to **Lakshmi**.
- **Athena (Minerva)** – Goddess of wisdom and strategy, resembling **Saraswati** in her role as a **protector of knowledge and civilization**.

3. Mesopotamia: Inanna/Ishtar – The Goddess of Love and War

- Inanna (also known as Ishtar in Babylonian mythology) was a **goddess of duality**—both love and destruction, much like **Kali**.
- She represented **death and rebirth, feminine power, and the cycle of creation**.

4. Mesoamerica: Coatlicue – The Serpent Mother

- The **Aztec goddess Coatlicue** was depicted as a **serpent-headed mother**, much like the Kundalini serpent.
- She represented **earth, fertility, and destruction**, showing the **cyclical nature of life**.

5. Celtic Traditions: The Triple Goddess

- The **Celtic Triple Goddess** (Maiden, Mother, Crone) reflects the **three phases of the feminine cycle**, just as Hinduism's Saraswati, Lakshmi, and Kali do.
- She was associated with the **moon, nature, and cycles of life and death**.

These diverse traditions reveal **a common truth**—the **Divine Feminine is universal**. Whether called Shakti, Isis, Inanna, or Gaia, she is the **creative force that sustains existence**.

---

4. The Suppression and Revival of Shakti Worship

Throughout history, patriarchal systems have often **suppressed** goddess traditions, diminishing the role of the Divine Feminine. However, in recent times, there has been a **global resurgence of feminine spirituality**:

- More people are rediscovering **Tantra, Kundalini Yoga, and Goddess worship**.
- Feminine wisdom is being honored in **healing practices, eco-spirituality, and sacred activism**.
- The world is moving toward **balancing masculine and feminine energies**, recognizing that true power comes from **harmony, not domination**.

Shakti is not confined to one religion, culture, or time period—**she is the eternal force that moves all things**. In Hinduism, Tantra, and global traditions, she has been revered as the **goddess, mother, protector, destroyer, and liberator**.

As we awaken to Shakti's presence in our own lives, we tap into **our highest potential**, becoming co-creators of our reality. Whether through meditation, devotion, or everyday awareness, we can **honor the Divine Feminine** and reclaim the **sacred balance of the universe**.

Kundalini is the **sacred energy of divine awakening**, the fire that transforms the ordinary into the extraordinary. It is **our connection to Shakti, to the universe, and to our highest self**.

Once awakened, it is impossible to return to life as before. Kundalini takes us on a journey of **deep transformation, healing, and spiritual evolution**, leading to the ultimate realization: **We are divine.**

The Cosmic Dance of Shiva and Shakti – The Union of Masculine and Feminine Energies

The **dance of Shiva and Shakti** is the eternal interplay between **consciousness and energy, stillness and motion, form and formlessness**. This divine union is not just a mythological concept—it is the foundation of the universe itself. In every aspect of life, from creation to destruction, from human relationships to cosmic expansion, Shiva and Shakti represent the **dual yet unified forces** that drive existence.

This chapter explores their **symbolism, philosophy, and spiritual significance**, and how we can integrate this understanding into our lives.

---

1. Who are Shiva and Shakti?

Shiva: The Pure Consciousness

Shiva represents **absolute stillness, awareness, and the unchanging reality**. He is:

- The **Supreme Consciousness** beyond time and space.
- The **eternal witness**, watching over creation without attachment.
- The force of **dissolution** that clears away illusion (*maya*), leading to enlightenment.

Shiva is often depicted as:

- A **meditating ascetic**, symbolizing pure awareness.
- **Nataraja, the Cosmic Dancer**, who dissolves the old to create the new.
- **Ardhanarishvara, the half-male, half-female form**, showing unity with Shakti.

Without Shakti, **Shiva is inert—like an ocean without waves, space without motion, a body without life**.

Shakti: The Divine Energy

Shakti is **the creative force that brings existence into motion**. She is:

- The **power of action, love, and transformation**.
- The **source of manifestation**—the material world arises through her.
- The **life force (prana)** that moves within all beings.

Shakti is depicted as:

- **Durga** – The warrior goddess who destroys ignorance.
- **Lakshmi** – The goddess of abundance, beauty, and prosperity.
- **Kali** – The fierce form of transformation, dissolving ego and illusion.

Without Shiva, **Shakti is chaotic energy without direction—like a river without a bed, fire without control, movement without purpose.**

Thus, **Shiva and Shakti are not separate**—they are two aspects of the **same cosmic reality**.

---

2. The Dance of Creation: Shiva and Shakti in the Universe

The **universe itself is born from the union of Shiva and Shakti**. In Hindu cosmology:

- Shiva is **pure potential**, and Shakti is **the activating force** that transforms that potential into reality.
- When Shiva and Shakti unite, the **cosmic dance of existence begins**.

This is beautifully represented in **Nataraja, the Dancing Shiva**, who performs the **Tandava dance**—a rhythmic play of **creation, preservation, and destruction**.

- **The Drum (Damaru)** – Creates sound, symbolizing **Shakti bringing forth creation**.
- **The Fire (Agni)** – Represents the **destructive aspect of Shakti**, dissolving old forms.
- **The Raised Foot** – Liberation (*moksha*), which is attained when **Shiva and Shakti unite within us**.

Thus, **all movement, cycles, and rhythms of life are a dance between these two cosmic forces**.

---

3. The Spiritual Meaning: Awakening Shiva and Shakti Within

For our free video kundalini training visit https://shiftnetwork.infusionsoft.com/go/akeg/a20331

Just as Shiva and Shakti exist in the cosmos, they also exist **within each of us**.

- **Shiva is our inner awareness, wisdom, and higher consciousness.**
- **Shakti is our passion, creativity, and life force energy.**

When they are in **balance**, we experience **wholeness, clarity, and deep fulfillment**. But when they are **out of balance**, life becomes unstable:

Shakti Dominates (Excess Energy, No Awareness)	Shiva Dominates (Awareness Without Action)
Overactivity, stress, chaos	Disconnection, detachment, stagnation
Emotionally reactive	Emotionally numb
Restless mind, unfocused desires	Lack of passion, absence of creativity

The goal of spiritual evolution is to **unite Shiva and Shakti within us**—to awaken **conscious energy and enlightened action**.

---

4. The Sacred Union: Tantra and Kundalini Awakening

In **Tantric philosophy**, the **union of Shiva and Shakti** is the key to enlightenment. This is experienced through **Kundalini Awakening**, where:

1. **Kundalini Shakti (Serpent Energy)**, dormant at the base of the spine, begins to rise.
2. As it ascends, it **activates the chakras**, clearing blockages and awakening divine consciousness.
3. When it reaches the **Sahasrara (Crown Chakra)**, it merges with Shiva, resulting in **spiritual awakening and self-realization**.

This process is cultivated through **Tantric practices**, including:

- **Mantra Chanting** (Sound vibrations that awaken energy).
- **Breathwork (Pranayama)** (Balancing life force energy).
- **Sacred Sexuality** (Harnessing energy for spiritual awakening).
- **Meditation** (Dissolving duality and experiencing oneness).

When Kundalini rises, **we experience the divine marriage of Shiva and Shakti within**—a state of **cosmic bliss, wisdom, and enlightenment**.

---

5. The Dance in Daily Life: Shiva and Shakti in Relationships

For our free chakra energy training course visit https://chakra.gr8.com/

The Shiva-Shakti dynamic is also reflected in **human relationships**—not just in romantic partnerships but in **all forms of interaction**.

Balanced Relationships (Sacred Union)

- **Both partners honor their masculine and feminine energies.**
- There is mutual **growth, love, and respect**.
- The relationship becomes a path to **higher consciousness**.

Unbalanced Relationships

Too Much Shakti (Energy Without Awareness)	Too Much Shiva (Awareness Without Connection)
Emotional chaos, drama, possessiveness	Disconnection, detachment, coldness
Over-dependence on external validation	Lack of passion, suppressed emotions
Unconscious reactions	Avoidance of emotional depth

The key to harmony in relationships is to **integrate both Shiva and Shakti within ourselves**—to balance **awareness and action, stillness and passion, independence and connection**.

---

6. The Ultimate Realization: The Non-Duality of Shiva and Shakti

At the highest level of realization, **Shiva and Shakti are one**. The great sages and mystics describe this as **Advaita (Non-Duality)**:

- There is no separation between **form (Shakti) and formlessness (Shiva)**.
- The entire universe is a **play of consciousness (Lila)**.
- True liberation (*moksha*) is the realization that **we are both Shiva and Shakti, eternal and ever-changing**.

The **dance of Shiva and Shakti** is the dance of **life itself**—a rhythm of expansion and contraction, creation and dissolution, stillness and motion.

When we understand this, we step into **flow, harmony, and divine presence**.

The **Cosmic Dance of Shiva and Shakti** is not just an external event—it is **happening within us at every moment**. By:

- **Awakening our consciousness (Shiva)**
- **Embracing our energy (Shakti)**
- **Balancing both in daily life**

...we step into **wholeness, love, and divine power**.

Ultimately, **Shiva and Shakti are YOU**—and their dance is the dance of your soul's journey.

The Triple Goddess – Saraswati, Lakshmi, and Kali as the Three Aspects of Shakti

Shakti, the Divine Feminine energy, is not a singular entity but manifests in multiple forms to fulfill different cosmic functions. In Hindu philosophy, she is often seen in her **Triple Goddess** aspect, where she embodies the three fundamental forces of the universe:

1. **Saraswati** – The Goddess of Wisdom and Creativity (*Jnana Shakti*)
2. **Lakshmi** – The Goddess of Abundance and Prosperity (*Iccha Shakti*)
3. **Kali (or Durga)** – The Goddess of Power and Transformation (*Kriya Shakti*)

Together, these three goddesses represent the complete cycle of **creation, preservation, and destruction**, demonstrating how feminine energy sustains and evolves the cosmos. This chapter explores the symbolism, spiritual significance, and practical ways to invoke these three forms of Shakti.

---

1. Saraswati – The Goddess of Wisdom and Creativity (*Jnana Shakti*)

Symbolism and Attributes

Saraswati is the embodiment of **knowledge, wisdom, arts, music, and learning**. She represents **Jnana Shakti**, the power of pure knowledge that illuminates the mind and soul.

She is typically depicted as:

- A **radiant goddess dressed in white**, sitting on a lotus, symbolizing purity and transcendence.
- Holding a **veena (musical instrument)**, representing creative expression and harmony.
- Holding **scriptures**, symbolizing wisdom and intellectual pursuits.
- Accompanied by a **swan**, which represents discernment—the ability to separate truth from illusion.

Spiritual Significance

Saraswati represents the **intellectual and creative force** that allows human civilization to flourish. She is the **source of speech, language, philosophy, and higher consciousness**. Without Saraswati, there is **ignorance, confusion, and lack of direction**.

Invoking Saraswati

- **Mantra**: *Om Aim Saraswatyai Namah* (Chanted for wisdom and clarity).
- **Practices**:
    - **Reading and studying spiritual texts** to cultivate wisdom.
    - **Writing, music, and creative pursuits** to express divine inspiration.
    - **Meditation on a white lotus or flowing water**, visualizing knowledge and clarity filling the mind.

Saraswati's energy is essential for **students, artists, writers, and seekers of truth**. She guides us toward enlightenment by sharpening our intellect and deepening our understanding.

---

2. Lakshmi – The Goddess of Prosperity and Abundance (*Iccha Shakti*)

Symbolism and Attributes

Lakshmi is the embodiment of **wealth, prosperity, beauty, fertility, and well-being**. She represents **Iccha Shakti**, the power of divine will and desire that sustains life.

She is depicted as:

- A **golden goddess seated on a lotus**, radiating grace and abundance.
- Showering **gold coins**, symbolizing material and spiritual wealth.
- Holding **lotuses**, representing purity, fortune, and growth.
- Accompanied by **elephants**, signifying power, wisdom, and stability.

Spiritual Significance

Lakshmi's energy is not just about **financial prosperity**—she represents **all forms of abundance**, including love, happiness, health, and spiritual wealth. Without her, there is **poverty, lack, and disharmony**.

She teaches that true wealth is not just external riches but **inner fulfillment and generosity**.

Invoking Lakshmi

- **Mantra**: *Om Shreem Mahalakshmyai Namah* (Chanted for prosperity and well-being).
- **Practices**:
    - **Acts of generosity** – Sharing wealth, kindness, and resources to invoke abundance.
    - **Maintaining beauty and cleanliness** in one's home and surroundings, as Lakshmi resides in places of harmony.
    - **Gratitude practice**, appreciating existing blessings to attract more abundance.

Lakshmi's blessings flow when we align with **self-worth, gratitude, and responsible wealth creation**.

---

3. Kali – The Goddess of Power and Transformation (*Kriya Shakti*)

Symbolism and Attributes

Kali is the embodiment of **raw power, destruction, time, and liberation**. She represents **Kriya Shakti**, the force of action and transformation that clears away illusion and ego.

She is depicted as:

- **Dark-skinned, wild-haired, and adorned with a garland of skulls**, symbolizing the destruction of ignorance.
- Holding a **sword**, which represents the severing of ego and attachment.
- Standing over **Shiva's body**, showing that without Shakti, even supreme consciousness (Shiva) is lifeless.
- With **a protruding tongue**, symbolizing the swallowing of illusions and falsehoods.

Spiritual Significance

Kali is the force of **death and rebirth**, breaking down all that is false so that truth may shine. She is the most **misunderstood goddess**, often seen as terrifying, but she is actually the most compassionate—**she destroys only what keeps us from liberation**.

Without Kali's energy, there is **stagnation, fear, and attachment to illusion**.

Invoking Kali

- **Mantra**: *Om Krim Kalikayai Namah* (Chanted for protection and transformation).
- **Practices**:

- **Facing fears and embracing change**, allowing old patterns to dissolve.
- **Meditating on darkness or fire**, visualizing negativity being burned away.
- **Surrendering to the divine flow**, trusting that destruction leads to rebirth.

Kali's energy is crucial in times of **deep transformation, personal growth, and overcoming inner demons**.

---

4. The Trinity of Shakti – How They Work Together

Saraswati, Lakshmi, and Kali Represent the Three Phases of Life

Goddess	Role in the Cycle of Life	Aspect of Shakti
Saraswati	Inspiration, learning, and creative ideas	*Jnana Shakti* (Wisdom Power)
Lakshmi	Manifestation, abundance, and preservation	*Iccha Shakti* (Will Power)
Kali	Transformation, destruction of the old, and rebirth	*Kriya Shakti* (Action Power)

- Saraswati **gives us knowledge and vision**.
- Lakshmi **nourishes and sustains us**.
- Kali **destroys illusions and liberates us**.

Just as nature **creates, sustains, and dissolves**, these three goddesses guide our **personal growth, relationships, and spiritual awakening**.

---

5. Integrating the Triple Goddess in Daily Life

To embody the power of Saraswati, Lakshmi, and Kali, we must:

- **Cultivate wisdom and clarity** (Saraswati) through learning and self-reflection.
- **Practice gratitude and generosity** (Lakshmi) by honoring abundance in all forms.
- **Embrace change and fearlessness** (Kali) by letting go of attachments and old patterns.

A balanced life requires all three aspects—**wisdom, abundance, and transformation**. By honoring these energies within us, we align with the **full spectrum of Shakti's divine power**.

The Role of the Divine Feminine in Healing – Restoring Balance in the Self and the World

Healing is the process of returning to wholeness—physically, emotionally, mentally, and spiritually. In many ancient traditions, the **Divine Feminine** is regarded as the ultimate healer, the nurturing force that restores balance in individuals and the collective.

The world today faces a profound imbalance, where **dominant masculine energies— focused on logic, competition, and control—often suppress the intuitive, compassionate, and cyclical nature of the feminine**. This disconnection has led to **stress, disease, ecological destruction, and emotional fragmentation**.

The return of the **Divine Feminine in healing** is not about rejecting masculine energy but about restoring balance. This chapter explores how Shakti, the sacred feminine energy, facilitates healing within the self, relationships, communities, and the planet.

---

1. Understanding the Divine Feminine as a Healing Force

The Divine Feminine, or **Shakti**, is the **primordial energy of creation, nourishment, and transformation**. This energy manifests in various ways:

- **As the nurturing mother** (*Maa Shakti*) – providing unconditional love and emotional safety.
- **As the wise healer** (*Saraswati, Dhanvantari, Isis*) – guiding us towards wisdom, balance, and self-awareness.
- **As the fierce protector** (*Kali, Durga*) – cutting through negativity and toxic patterns that block healing.
- **As the sensual and creative force** (*Lakshmi, Aphrodite*) – inspiring beauty, pleasure, and self-love.

In healing, the Divine Feminine works through **intuition, emotional intelligence, receptivity, and connection to nature**. She reminds us that **true healing is holistic, addressing body, mind, and spirit together**.

---

2. Healing the Self – Reconnecting with Inner Shakti

Healing begins within. When we are disconnected from our **inner Divine Feminine**, we experience:

- **Emotional suppression** – ignoring feelings, leading to stress and burnout.
- **Disconnection from intuition** – relying only on logic, which causes imbalance.
- **Neglect of the body's wisdom** – ignoring rest, nourishment, and self-care.

- **Fear of vulnerability** – suppressing authenticity and emotional openness.

How to Invoke the Divine Feminine for Personal Healing

1. **Inner Nourishment (Self-Care and Rest)**
   - Honor **cycles of rest and renewal** instead of pushing through exhaustion.
   - Practice **self-care rituals** like herbal baths, massage, and conscious eating.
   - Listen to your **body's wisdom**—slow down when needed.

2. **Emotional Healing (Releasing and Receiving)**
   - Allow yourself to **feel emotions fully** without judgment.
   - Work with the **heart chakra** to cultivate compassion and forgiveness.
   - Practice **womb healing** or **sacral chakra work** to release past trauma.

3. **Connecting with Intuition (Deep Listening and Awareness)**
   - Engage in **meditation and breathwork** to attune to your inner voice.
   - Work with **moon cycles** to align with natural rhythms.
   - Use **dream journaling and divination (tarot, pendulums)** to deepen intuition.

4. **Sacred Creativity (Expressing Shakti Through Art and Movement)**
   - Dance, paint, sing—use creative outlets to **release emotions and energies**.
   - Explore **feminine movement practices** like belly dancing or yoga.
   - Write poetry or journal to tap into deeper emotions and insights.

When we **restore balance within**, we radiate healing to others and become a vessel for divine wisdom.

---

3. Healing Relationships – Restoring Sacred Union

Just as the Divine Feminine brings balance within, she also restores harmony in **relationships**. Many relationships suffer because of an **imbalance between masculine and feminine energies**:

Imbalance in Feminine Energy	Imbalance in Masculine Energy
Over-giving, people-pleasing	Emotional suppression, lack of empathy

Imbalance in Feminine Energy	Imbalance in Masculine Energy
Lack of boundaries	Over-controlling, competitive behavior
Emotional instability	Disconnection from feelings and intuition
Fear of speaking truth	Fear of vulnerability

How to Heal Relationships Through the Divine Feminine

- **Embrace Emotional Authenticity** – Communicate with openness and vulnerability.
- **Practice Deep Listening and Receptivity** – Hold space for others without judgment.
- **Create Balance in Giving and Receiving** – Don't overextend; allow support from others.
- **Bring Ritual into Relationships** – Share sacred practices like **meditation, dance, or nature walks**.

When relationships are infused with **Shakti energy**, they become **nurturing, harmonious, and deeply fulfilling**.

---

4. Healing the Collective – The Return of Feminine Consciousness

The **Divine Feminine is rising** in the collective consciousness, bringing healing to:

1. Women's Empowerment

For centuries, **feminine wisdom was suppressed**—women were denied spiritual and leadership roles, and their voices were silenced. The return of Shakti calls for:

- **Honoring feminine leadership** based on intuition, compassion, and collaboration.
- **Healing generational trauma** from patriarchal oppression.
- **Restoring sacred feminine traditions** (womb wisdom, goddess worship, sisterhood circles).

2. Restoring Connection to Mother Earth (Gaia Shakti)

The Divine Feminine is deeply connected to **nature**. The modern world's separation from the earth has led to environmental destruction. Healing requires:

- **Reconnecting with nature** – honoring the elements, forests, rivers, and animals.

For our free video kundalini training visit https://shiftnetwork.infusionsoft.com/go/akeg/a20331

- **Eco-conscious living** – sustainable choices, ethical consumption, and regenerative farming.
- **Rituals of gratitude** – offerings to the earth, moon ceremonies, and sacred land practices.

3. Healing the World Through Compassion and Unity

The world is in **crisis due to dominance-based, competitive structures**. The Divine Feminine brings balance by:

- Promoting **cooperation instead of competition**.
- Cultivating **peaceful conflict resolution** over aggression.
- Encouraging **heart-centered leadership in politics, business, and spirituality**.

By **honoring feminine wisdom**, we heal not just individuals but entire communities and societies.

---

5. The Integration of Divine Masculine and Feminine

Healing is not about **rejecting masculine energy** but about **creating balance**. The Divine Feminine and Divine Masculine must work together to:

Divine Feminine (Shakti) Divine Masculine (Shiva)

Divine Feminine (Shakti)	Divine Masculine (Shiva)
Intuition	Logic
Emotion	Rationality
Compassion	Strength
Receptivity	Action
Flow	Structure

When these energies are integrated:

- **Women reclaim their power without suppressing their softness.**
- **Men embrace emotions and intuition without losing strength.**
- **Society moves from dominance to balance, from control to harmony.**

Healing is about **becoming whole**—individually and collectively.

To truly **restore balance in the self and the world**, we must **embody** the Divine Feminine. This means:

For our free chakra energy training course visit https://chakra.gr8.com/

- **Honoring the wisdom of the body, emotions, and intuition.**
- **Healing relationships by embracing sacred feminine values.**
- **Reconnecting with nature and living in harmony with the planet.**
- **Balancing masculine and feminine energies within ourselves.**

By doing this, we become **vessels of healing, love, and transformation**. The return of the Divine Feminine is not a future event—it is **happening now, within each of us**.

Part II: Understanding Kundalini Energy

The Serpent Power – The Coiled Energy at the Base of the Spine

The concept of **Kundalini Shakti**, often referred to as the **Serpent Power**, is central to many mystical traditions, especially **Tantra, Yoga, and Vedantic philosophy**. It represents the **latent divine energy** coiled at the base of the spine, waiting to be awakened and directed upward through the chakras to bring about **spiritual enlightenment and transformation**.

This chapter explores the **origins, significance, process of awakening, and effects of Kundalini energy**, as well as its role in **personal and cosmic evolution**.

---

1. What is Kundalini Shakti?

Meaning and Symbolism

- The term **Kundalini** derives from the Sanskrit word *"kundal,"* meaning "coiled" or "circular," referring to the way this energy lies **dormant like a serpent** at the base of the spine.
- In spiritual traditions, the **serpent** is a symbol of **primordial energy, transformation, and wisdom**.
- This energy is **Shakti**, the **Divine Feminine force of creation**, lying in its potential form until activated.

The Connection Between Kundalini and Consciousness

- In its dormant state, **Kundalini energy is asleep in the Muladhara (Root Chakra)**, maintaining the basic survival functions of life.
- When awakened, **it rises through the central energy channel (Sushumna Nadi), activating each chakra**, leading to higher states of awareness.
- The ultimate goal of Kundalini awakening is **self-realization (Moksha)**—the union of **Shakti (dynamic energy)** and **Shiva (pure consciousness)** at the crown chakra.

---

2. The Anatomy of Kundalini – Nadis, Chakras, and Prana

To understand Kundalini energy, we must explore the **subtle energy system** within the human body:

1. The Three Primary Nadis (Energy Channels)

The **Nadis** are energy pathways that conduct **Prana (life force energy)** throughout the body. The three most significant ones are:

- **Ida Nadi (Left Channel)** – Associated with the **moon, feminine energy, intuition, and emotions**. Governs the left side of the body.
- **Pingala Nadi (Right Channel)** – Associated with the **sun, masculine energy, logic, and action**. Governs the right side of the body.
- **Sushumna Nadi (Central Channel)** – The **main spiritual channel** where Kundalini rises when activated. This **pathway leads to enlightenment**.

When Kundalini is dormant, **Ida and Pingala dominate, keeping human consciousness focused on duality (ego, desires, emotions, and intellect)**. But when **Kundalini rises through Sushumna, it transcends duality**, leading to unity and higher awareness.

2. The Seven Chakras and Their Role in Awakening

As Kundalini ascends, it activates the **seven chakras**, each representing a level of consciousness:

Chakra	Location	Aspect of Awakening
Muladhara (Root)	Base of spine	Survival, grounding, stability
Swadhisthana (Sacral)	Below navel	Creativity, sexuality, emotions
Manipura (Solar Plexus)	Stomach area	Personal power, will, transformation
Anahata (Heart)	Center of chest	Love, compassion, emotional balance
Vishuddha (Throat)	Throat	Expression, truth, communication
Ajna (Third Eye)	Between eyebrows	Intuition, inner wisdom, vision
Sahasrara (Crown)	Top of head	Pure consciousness, divine union

When Kundalini **fully awakens and reaches the Crown Chakra**, it dissolves the ego, bringing **self-realization, enlightenment, and blissful union with the Divine**.

---

3. The Process of Kundalini Awakening

1. Signs of Dormant Kundalini Energy

Before Kundalini awakens, one may feel:

- A sense of **inner restlessness or longing for deeper meaning**.

- Strong **intuitive abilities and spiritual curiosity**.
- Frequent **synchronicities and mystical experiences**.

2. Ways Kundalini Awakens

Kundalini can be activated in different ways:

A. Spontaneous Awakening

- Can happen unexpectedly due to **past life karma, deep meditation, trauma, or near-death experiences**.
- Often **intense and overwhelming**, leading to temporary **spiritual crisis or ego death**.

B. Gradual Awakening (Yogic Practices)

- More stable and manageable. Methods include:
    - **Mantra Chanting** (*Om Namah Shivaya*, Kundalini bija mantras).
    - **Breathwork (Pranayama)** – Such as *Nadi Shodhana* (alternate nostril breathing) and *Kapalabhati*.
    - **Meditation on Chakras** – Visualizing energy moving up the spine.
    - **Shaktipat** (Energy transmission from a Guru).
    - **Tantric and Bhakti Practices** – Using devotion and rituals to awaken Shakti.

---

4. The Effects of Kundalini Awakening

Kundalini awakening brings **profound transformation** on all levels:

Physical Effects

- **Heat or energy surges** in the spine and body.
- Spontaneous **yoga postures (Kriyas) or mudras**.
- **Increased vitality** or moments of exhaustion.

Emotional and Psychological Effects

- **Old traumas resurface** to be healed.
- Heightened **emotional sensitivity and empathy**.
- Phases of **bliss, love, or deep emptiness** as the ego dissolves.

Spiritual and Mystical Effects

For our free video kundalini training visit https://shiftnetwork.infusionsoft.com/go/akeg/a20331

- **Enhanced intuition and extrasensory perception.**
- **Deep states of meditation and oneness with the universe.**
- A sense of **divine presence and unconditional love.**

---

5. Challenges and Dangers of Kundalini Awakening

While Kundalini is a powerful force of transformation, **awakening it prematurely or without guidance can lead to difficulties.**

1. Common Challenges

- **Emotional overwhelm** – Old wounds resurface suddenly.
- **Physical discomfort** – Energy blockages may cause headaches, heart palpitations, or digestive issues.
- **Spiritual Ego** – Mistaking Kundalini experiences for superiority or divine status.

2. How to Navigate a Safe Awakening

- **Grounding practices** – Spending time in nature, eating nourishing food, and engaging in physical activities.
- **Surrender to the process** – Trusting that everything is unfolding as it should.
- **Seeking guidance** – Learning from **spiritual teachers, healers, or mentors** who understand Kundalini energy.

---

6. The Divine Union – Kundalini and the Cosmic Dance of Shiva and Shakti

The journey of Kundalini is the **reunion of Shakti (Divine Feminine) and Shiva (Divine Masculine).**

- **Shakti (energy) rises** from the base of the spine, seeking **Shiva (pure consciousness) at the crown.**
- When they unite, **duality dissolves, and one experiences supreme bliss, enlightenment, and liberation (Moksha).**

Kundalini awakening is **the most powerful spiritual transformation** available to a human being. It is the path to:

- **Expanded consciousness** and direct connection to the Divine.
- **Healing on all levels**—physical, emotional, and spiritual.

For our free chakra energy training course visit https://chakra.gr8.com/

- The realization of one's highest potential.

The Subtle Body – Nadis, Chakras, and the Energy Pathways

The human being is not just a **physical entity** but a complex **multidimensional system** of energy and consciousness. In many ancient spiritual traditions, especially **Tantra, Yoga, and Vedanta**, the **subtle body** (*sukshma sharira*) is recognized as the intermediary between the **physical body (sthula sharira) and the causal body (karana sharira), which holds the soul's divine essence**.

The **subtle body** contains **Nadis (energy channels), Chakras (energy centers), and Prana (life force energy)**. These components regulate our **spiritual, emotional, mental, and physical well-being**. Understanding and working with them helps in **awakening higher consciousness and self-realization**.

---

1. The Three Layers of Human Existence

Before diving into the **subtle body**, it's important to understand the **three bodies** in yogic philosophy:

1. **Physical Body (Sthula Sharira)**
    - The tangible, material form made of flesh, bones, and organs.
    - It is nourished by food, exercise, and sleep.
    - This is the **grossest** level of existence.

2. **Subtle Body (Sukshma Sharira)**
    - The **energy and mind body**, consisting of **thoughts, emotions, chakras, nadis, and prana (life force)**.
    - It is **more refined** than the physical body and is affected by meditation, breathwork, and emotions.

3. **Causal Body (Karana Sharira)**
    - The **deepest layer of consciousness**, containing **past life karmas and the blueprint of the soul**.
    - It is beyond **mental and physical awareness** and is connected to **divine wisdom and enlightenment**.

The **subtle body acts as the bridge** between the **physical and spiritual realms**, influencing health, intuition, and spiritual evolution.

For our free video kundalini training visit https://shiftnetwork.infusionsoft.com/go/akeg/a20331

2. The Nadis – The Energy Channels of the Body

What Are Nadis?

Nadi (Sanskrit: *nāḍī*) means **"flow" or "channel."** These are **energetic pathways** through which **prana (life force energy) circulates** in the subtle body.

According to yogic scriptures, there are **72,000 nadis**, but three are the most significant:

1. The Three Primary Nadis

Nadi	Flow	Symbolism	Effects
Ida Nadi	Left side of the spine	Lunar, Feminine, Intuition, Emotions	Cooling, calming, associated with the parasympathetic nervous system
Pingala Nadi	Right side of the spine	Solar, Masculine, Logic, Action	Warming, energizing, associated with the sympathetic nervous system
Sushumna Nadi	Central energy channel along the spine	The path of spiritual awakening	When active, it leads to **enlightenment and self-realization**

Ida and Pingala: The Dance of Duality

- **Ida Nadi** represents the **Divine Feminine (Shakti)** – intuition, receptivity, emotions.
- **Pingala Nadi** represents the **Divine Masculine (Shiva)** – logic, action, discipline.
- **When these two are balanced, Sushumna activates**, leading to **spiritual transformation**.

The Role of Nadis in Kundalini Awakening

- **When Kundalini awakens, it travels through Sushumna Nadi**, activating each chakra along the way.
- This leads to **expanded consciousness, self-realization, and enlightenment**.

---

3. The Seven Chakras – The Energy Centers of the Body

What Are Chakras?

Chakras (*Sanskrit: "wheel"*) are **energy centers** that regulate the **flow of prana** in the body. Each chakra governs specific **physical, emotional, and spiritual functions**.

The Seven Main Chakras

For our free chakra energy training course visit https://chakra.gr8.com/

Chakra	Location	Element	Function	When Balanced	When Blocked
Muladhara (Root Chakra)	Base of spine	Earth	Survival, grounding, stability	Secure, strong foundation	Fear, insecurity, instability
Swadhisthana (Sacral Chakra)	Below navel	Water	Creativity, emotions, pleasure	Passion, flow, emotional balance	Guilt, lack of creativity, repression
Manipura (Solar Plexus Chakra)	Stomach	Fire	Personal power, confidence, will	Strong self-esteem, transformation	Powerlessness, low self-worth
Anahata (Heart Chakra)	Center of chest	Air	Love, compassion, relationships	Unconditional love, emotional healing	Jealousy, grief, resentment
Vishuddha (Throat Chakra)	Throat	Ether	Communication, truth, self-expression	Authenticity, clear speech	Fear of speaking, dishonesty
Ajna (Third Eye Chakra)	Between eyebrows	Light	Intuition, wisdom, insight	Clarity, heightened perception	Confusion, lack of direction
Sahasrara (Crown Chakra)	Top of head	Consciousness	Divine connection, enlightenment	Oneness, divine bliss	Spiritual disconnection, cynicism

The Role of Chakras in Kundalini Awakening

- As **Kundalini energy rises through each chakra**, it **activates different levels of consciousness**.
- When all chakras are **open and aligned**, one experiences **self-realization, deep inner peace, and cosmic unity**.

---

4. Prana – The Life Force That Flows Through the Subtle Body

What Is Prana?

- **Prana** (*Sanskrit: "vital force"*) is the **energy that sustains life**.

- It moves through **Nadis and Chakras**, powering our **thoughts, emotions, and spiritual connection**.

Types of Prana

Prana manifests in **five different energies (Pancha Prana Vayus)**:

Prana Vayu	Function	Location
Prana	Inhalation, life force intake	Chest
Apana	Excretion, downward energy	Pelvis
Samana	Digestion, transformation	Navel
Udana	Speech, upward movement	Throat
Vyana	Circulation, expansion	Whole body

How to Cultivate and Balance Prana

- **Pranayama (Breathwork)** – *Alternate Nostril Breathing (Nadi Shodhana), Kapalabhati, Bhastrika* to clear energy pathways.
- **Meditation and Mantra Chanting** – Activates chakras and harmonizes pranic flow.
- **Yoga Asanas** – Helps release energy blockages.
- **Diet and Lifestyle** – Eating sattvic (pure) foods, maintaining mindfulness, and avoiding stress increases pranic energy.

---

5. How to Harmonize the Subtle Body for Spiritual Awakening

Daily Practices for Balancing Nadis and Chakras

- **Morning Breathwork (Pranayama)** – Balances **Ida and Pingala** to awaken **Sushumna**.
- **Chakra Meditation** – Visualizing light in each chakra.
- **Mantra Chanting** – Bija (seed) mantras like *OM, LAM, VAM, RAM, YAM, HAM, AUM* activate chakras.
- **Grounding Activities** – Walking barefoot, being in nature.
- **Sacred Movement** – Yoga, dance, or Tai Chi to stimulate energy flow.

---

6. Conclusion – Becoming One with the Subtle Body

For our free video kundalini training visit https://shiftnetwork.infusionsoft.com/go/akeg/a20331

By understanding and working with the **Nadis, Chakras, and Prana**, we can:
- ☑ **Balance our emotions and mind**
- ☑ **Enhance intuition and spiritual awareness**
- ☑ **Unblock energy flow for vitality and inner peace**
- ☑ **Prepare for Kundalini Awakening and Enlightenment**

The Seven Chakras and Kundalini Awakening – Their Roles in Spiritual Transformation

The **seven chakras** are the primary **energy centers** of the **subtle body**, each governing different aspects of **physical, emotional, mental, and spiritual well-being**. In yogic philosophy, the chakras serve as **gateways to higher consciousness**, and their activation leads to **Kundalini Awakening**, the **spiritual evolution of the soul**.

When **Kundalini Shakti**, the **dormant divine energy** at the base of the spine, is awakened, it rises through the **Sushumna Nadi**, activating each chakra along the way. This journey transforms one's **awareness, energy, and perception**, ultimately leading to **self-realization and enlightenment**.

---

1. Understanding the Seven Chakras

Each **chakra (Sanskrit: "wheel" or "disk")** is an **energy vortex** that regulates pranic flow. Below is an overview of their **locations, elements, and roles in spiritual transformation**.

Chakra	Location	Element	Function	Awakening Effect	Bija Mantra
Muladhara (Root Chakra)	Base of spine	Earth	Stability, survival, grounding	Fearlessness, security, connection to nature	**LAM**
Swadhisthana (Sacral Chakra)	Below navel	Water	Creativity, pleasure, emotions	Emotional balance, enhanced intuition, sexual transmutation	**VAM**
Manipura (Solar Plexus Chakra)	Stomach	Fire	Willpower, confidence, transformation	Inner strength, personal power, charisma	**RAM**

For our free chakra energy training course visit https://chakra.gr8.com/

Chakra	Location	Element	Function	Awakening Effect	Bija Mantra
Anahata (Heart Chakra)	Center of chest	Air	Love, compassion, relationships	Unconditional love, forgiveness, selflessness	YAM
Vishuddha (Throat Chakra)	Throat	Ether	Communication, truth, self-expression	Pure speech, divine communication, inner truth	HAM
Ajna (Third Eye Chakra)	Between eyebrows	Light	Intuition, wisdom, spiritual insight	Clairvoyance, higher consciousness, deep intuition	OM
Sahasrara (Crown Chakra)	Top of head	Consciousness	Divine connection, enlightenment	Liberation, unity with the Divine, cosmic awareness	Silent OM

Each chakra corresponds to **specific qualities, emotions, and levels of awareness**. As Kundalini rises, it **clears energetic blockages, purifies karma, and unlocks the highest human potential**.

2. Kundalini Awakening and Chakra Activation

What is Kundalini Awakening?

Kundalini is the **coiled serpent energy** at the **base of the spine**. When activated, it **travels up the Sushumna Nadi**, unlocking each **chakra's spiritual gifts**.

The Path of Awakening Through the Chakras

1. Muladhara (Root Chakra) – The Foundation of Awakening

- **Blocked by:** Fear, insecurity, instability.
- **Awakening Effect:**
    - Feeling **safe, grounded, and fearless**.
    - Greater **connection to the Earth and physical reality**.
- **Kundalini Activation:**
    - **Shaking sensations in the spine**, heat rising from the base.

2. Swadhisthana (Sacral Chakra) – The Flow of Energy

- **Blocked by:** Guilt, sexual repression, emotional suppression.
- **Awakening Effect:**
    - Creativity **unleashed**, heightened **pleasure and joy**.
    - Emotional **purification** and balance.
- **Kundalini Activation:**
    - Increased **passion, artistic inspiration, and spiritual sexuality**.

3. Manipura (Solar Plexus Chakra) – The Fire of Transformation

- **Blocked by:** Low self-esteem, doubt, lack of confidence.
- **Awakening Effect:**
    - Increased **self-discipline, willpower, and personal power**.
    - Ability to **manifest desires into reality**.
- **Kundalini Activation:**
    - A sense of **empowerment, motivation, and deep transformation**.

4. Anahata (Heart Chakra) – The Power of Love

- **Blocked by:** Grief, resentment, lack of love.
- **Awakening Effect:**
    - **Unconditional love** for all beings.
    - Deep compassion, emotional healing.
- **Kundalini Activation:**
    - Feeling of **divine love, intense heart expansion, blissful ecstasy**.

5. Vishuddha (Throat Chakra) – The Voice of Truth

- **Blocked by:** Lies, suppressed self-expression, fear of judgment.
- **Awakening Effect:**
    - Speaking **truth with clarity and confidence**.
    - Channeling **divine messages and creativity**.
- **Kundalini Activation:**
    - Spontaneous **mantra chanting, sound vibrations, clearer expression**.

6. Ajna (Third Eye Chakra) – The Awakening of Wisdom

- **Blocked by:** Illusions, lack of intuition, mental confusion.
- **Awakening Effect:**
    - **Heightened intuition, clarity, and spiritual visions.**
    - Direct perception of **divine realities and past lives**.
- **Kundalini Activation:**
    - Increased **psychic abilities, deep insights, synchronicities**.

7. Sahasrara (Crown Chakra) – The Final Liberation

- **Blocked by:** Ego, attachment, separation from the Divine.
- **Awakening Effect:**
    - **Oneness with the universe**, ultimate bliss.
    - Experience of **Samadhi (Divine Union)**.
- **Kundalini Activation:**
    - Pure **consciousness, cosmic awareness, loss of the "self" into divine light**.

When Kundalini **fully ascends to the Crown**, the seeker attains **self-realization, divine knowledge, and eternal bliss**.

---

3. Signs and Symptoms of Kundalini Awakening

As **Kundalini activates the chakras**, it produces various **physical, emotional, and spiritual effects**:

Physical Symptoms

- ✅ **Heat or energy surges** in the spine.
- ✅ **Tingling, vibrations, spontaneous movements (Kriyas)**.
- ✅ **Increased sensory perception, vivid dreams, and lucid visions**.

Emotional Symptoms

- ✅ **Sudden emotional releases** (joy, fear, anger, ecstasy).
- ✅ **Profound feelings of love and interconnectedness**.
- ✅ **Periods of intense bliss and deep emptiness**.

Spiritual Symptoms

For our free video kundalini training visit https://shiftnetwork.infusionsoft.com/go/akeg/a20331

- ☑ Heightened intuition and extrasensory perception.
- ☑ Synchronicities and divine signs.
- ☑ States of deep meditation, divine guidance, and mystical experiences.

4. How to Awaken and Balance the Chakras for Kundalini Activation

1. Pranayama (Breathwork)

- **Nadi Shodhana (Alternate Nostril Breathing):** Balances **Ida and Pingala** to activate **Sushumna Nadi**.
- **Bhastrika & Kapalabhati:** Energizes the chakras and awakens **Kundalini Shakti**.

2. Meditation and Visualization

- **Focusing on each chakra while chanting its Bija Mantra.**
- **Visualizing light rising up the spine.**

3. Yoga Asanas for Chakra Activation

- **Muladhara:** Tree Pose, Warrior Pose.
- **Swadhisthana:** Hip-opening poses (Butterfly, Pigeon Pose).
- **Manipura:** Core-strengthening poses (Boat Pose).
- **Anahata:** Heart-opening poses (Camel, Cobra Pose).
- **Vishuddha:** Shoulder Stand, Fish Pose.
- **Ajna:** Child's Pose, Meditation.
- **Sahasrara:** Lotus Pose, Headstand.

4. Chanting and Sound Healing

- Reciting **OM** and chakra mantras helps in deep **energetic cleansing**.

The journey of **Kundalini and the Chakras** is the **path to enlightenment**. As we open each chakra, we transcend **fear, ego, and illusion**, leading to **pure awareness and unity with the Divine**.

Signs and Symptoms of Awakening – Physical, Emotional, and Mystical Experiences

The awakening of **Kundalini** is a profound spiritual experience that can bring about various **signs and symptoms**. These manifestations may vary significantly among

For our free chakra energy training course visit https://chakra.gr8.com/

individuals, depending on their unique spiritual journey and readiness. Generally, these signs can be categorized into **physical, emotional, and mystical experiences**. Understanding these signs is crucial for navigating the awakening process with awareness and acceptance.

1. Physical Symptoms

A. Energy Sensations

- **Tingling or Vibrations:** Many individuals report **tingling sensations** in the spine, limbs, or throughout the body as **Kundalini energy** begins to awaken.
- **Heat or Warmth:** A feeling of warmth or heat may rise from the base of the spine up to the head, often described as a **warm current** or **electric energy**.

B. Movement and Spontaneity

- **Spontaneous Body Movements (Kriyas):** Individuals may experience **uncontrollable movements** such as shaking, swaying, or dancing. These movements are often seen as a means for the body to release energy blockages.
- **Postures and Asanas:** Some may find themselves naturally moving into specific yoga postures or **mudras** (hand gestures) without conscious intention.

C. Sensory Enhancements

- **Heightened Sensitivity:** Increased sensitivity to light, sound, touch, and even tastes is common. Some individuals may find themselves overwhelmed by sensory input.
- **Altered Perception of Time and Space:** The experience of time may feel distorted, and some may perceive space differently, feeling a sense of expansiveness or confinement.

D. Physical Changes

- **Changes in Sleep Patterns:** Sleep disturbances, such as insomnia or intense dreaming, are common. Some individuals may require less sleep, while others experience **vivid dreams** or nightmares.
- **Physical Ailments or Discomfort:** Temporary discomfort or **symptoms resembling illness** may arise as the body adjusts to the energetic shifts, including headaches, fatigue, or muscle tension.

2. Emotional Symptoms

A. Intense Emotions

- **Emotional Releases:** During awakening, individuals may experience **sudden and intense emotional releases**, including joy, grief, anger, or frustration. These releases are often cathartic and part of the healing process.
- **Heightened Sensitivity:** Emotions may feel **amplified**, leading to moments of deep empathy, compassion, or even overwhelming sadness.

B. Mood Swings

- **Fluctuating Emotions:** Individuals may experience rapid shifts in mood, going from extreme joy to profound sadness or anxiety. These fluctuations are often linked to energetic changes.
- **Fear and Anxiety:** As one confronts deeper truths about themselves and their past, feelings of fear or anxiety may surface, particularly related to unresolved issues or traumas.

C. Sense of Release and Freedom

- **Letting Go:** Awakening often encourages individuals to **release attachments** to unhealthy patterns, relationships, or beliefs, resulting in feelings of freedom and relief.
- **Deepening Self-Acceptance:** A growing acceptance of oneself, including flaws and strengths, can lead to enhanced self-love and confidence.

---

3. Mystical Experiences

A. Expanded Consciousness

- **Heightened Awareness:** A profound sense of awareness and presence often accompanies awakening. Individuals may feel deeply connected to their surroundings and more attuned to the energies of others.
- **Profound Insights:** Sudden flashes of insight or clarity about life, purpose, or the nature of reality may arise. These insights can be life-changing and transformative.

B. Spiritual Experiences

- **Intuitive Knowledge:** Enhanced intuition, psychic abilities, or foresight may develop during this period, leading to a greater understanding of oneself and others.
- **Connection with the Divine:** A deep sense of connection to the divine or universal consciousness is common. This can manifest as feelings of unconditional love, oneness, or the presence of divine beings.

C. Synchronicities

- **Meaningful Coincidences:** Many individuals notice an increase in **synchronicities**—meaningful coincidences that feel like signs or messages from the universe, guiding them along their spiritual path.
- **Signs and Symbols:** Repeated encounters with specific symbols, numbers, or animals can indicate a spiritual message or guidance relevant to the individual's journey.

D. Experiences of Oneness

- **Unity with All:** A profound sense of interconnectedness and unity with all living beings can occur, leading to feelings of deep compassion and empathy for others.
- **States of Bliss or Ecstasy:** Some individuals experience intense feelings of joy, bliss, or ecstasy during awakening, often described as a **state of pure love or divine bliss**.

4. Navigating the Awakening Process

While the signs and symptoms of Kundalini awakening can be both exhilarating and challenging, it's essential to approach the experience with **awareness and self-care**:

A. Grounding Practices

- Engage in grounding activities such as **walking barefoot**, spending time in nature, or practicing **yoga** to anchor oneself during intense energetic experiences.

B. Breathwork and Meditation

- **Pranayama (breathwork)** can help regulate energy flow, while **meditation** provides a space for reflection, integration, and calm.

C. Seek Support

- Connecting with a spiritual teacher, therapist, or supportive community can provide guidance and reassurance during the awakening process.

D. Embrace the Journey

- Accepting the experience as part of personal growth is vital. Journaling can be helpful for processing emotions and insights that arise during awakening.

Kundalini awakening is a transformative journey that often manifests through a wide array of **physical, emotional, and mystical signs**. Understanding these symptoms allows individuals to navigate their experiences with **greater awareness and**

acceptance. Embracing the awakening journey ultimately leads to profound personal and spiritual growth, offering the opportunity to realize one's true nature and potential.

The Challenges of Kundalini Rising – Navigating Crises and Spiritual Purges

Kundalini awakening is often described as a transformative spiritual journey that can lead to profound growth and enlightenment. However, this process can also bring about significant challenges, including **crises and spiritual purges**. Understanding these challenges is essential for navigating the awakening journey with resilience and self-awareness.

1. Understanding Kundalini Rising

Kundalini is the dormant **spiritual energy** believed to reside at the base of the spine. When awakened, it rises through the **Sushumna Nadi**, activating the chakras and facilitating spiritual growth. While this awakening can lead to heightened states of consciousness and personal transformation, it can also trigger **intense challenges**, often referred to as **Kundalini crises** or **spiritual purges**.

2. Common Challenges During Kundalini Rising

A. Physical Discomfort

- **Energetic Symptoms:** As Kundalini energy rises, individuals may experience physical symptoms such as **tremors, shaking, heat, or intense sensations** in various parts of the body.
- **Fatigue and Exhaustion:** The body may require significant rest as it adapts to the new energetic shifts, leading to periods of fatigue or lethargy.
- **Nausea or Digestive Issues:** Some may experience **nausea**, bloating, or other gastrointestinal discomfort as the energy moves through the body and clears blockages.

B. Emotional Turmoil

- **Intense Emotional Releases:** Awakening can lead to sudden and intense emotional upheavals, including grief, anger, fear, or joy. These emotional releases can feel overwhelming and may require processing and integration.
- **Mood Swings:** Individuals may experience rapid fluctuations in mood, which can be disorienting and lead to feelings of instability.

- **Anxiety and Fear:** The process may bring unresolved fears or anxieties to the surface, creating a sense of panic or existential crisis as one confronts deeper truths about themselves and their life.

C. Mental Challenges

- **Confusion and Disorientation:** As consciousness expands, individuals may feel disoriented or confused about their identity, purpose, or reality. This mental turmoil can lead to feelings of isolation or alienation.
- **Overactive Mind:** Increased mental activity, including racing thoughts or heightened perception, can lead to difficulty concentrating or staying grounded.
- **Crisis of Beliefs:** Awakening can challenge deeply held beliefs or worldviews, leading to a **spiritual crisis** as individuals reevaluate their understanding of reality and existence.

D. Spiritual Purges

- **Releasing Past Trauma:** The awakening process often brings unresolved traumas or emotional baggage to the surface for healing. This release can be painful and may require deep inner work to process and integrate.
- **Clearing Energy Blockages:** The rising Kundalini energy can forcefully clear energetic blockages, which may manifest as emotional purges or intense releases. This process can feel like a **cleansing storm**, bringing both catharsis and discomfort.
- **Detoxification:** Just as the body may go through a physical detox, spiritual purging can manifest as the release of negative thought patterns, attachments, or unhealthy habits.

---

3. Navigating Crises and Spiritual Purges

A. Grounding Practices

- **Connect with Nature:** Spending time in nature can help ground and stabilize energy, allowing individuals to reconnect with the Earth and regain a sense of balance.
- **Mindfulness and Breathwork:** Practicing mindfulness and deep breathing can help anchor awareness and calm the nervous system during overwhelming experiences.

B. Self-Care and Rest

- **Prioritize Rest:** Allowing for adequate rest and self-care is crucial during intense periods of awakening. Listening to the body's needs can help prevent burnout.

- **Healthy Lifestyle Choices:** Maintaining a balanced diet, staying hydrated, and engaging in gentle physical activity (such as yoga or walking) can support physical and energetic well-being.

C. Emotional Support

- **Journaling:** Writing about thoughts and emotions can facilitate processing and understanding of the experiences during awakening.
- **Seek Support:** Connecting with trusted friends, spiritual mentors, or support groups can provide guidance and reassurance during difficult times.

D. Energy Healing and Practices

- **Yoga and Movement:** Engaging in yoga or other forms of movement can help facilitate the flow of energy and release physical tension.
- **Meditation and Visualization:** Regular meditation can cultivate inner peace, allowing individuals to observe their experiences without becoming overwhelmed. Visualization techniques can also help direct energy and intention.

E. Embrace the Journey

- **Accept the Process:** Recognizing that challenges are a natural part of the Kundalini journey can foster acceptance and resilience. Embracing the ups and downs as part of spiritual growth can lead to deeper insights and transformation.
- **Focus on Integration:** Allowing time for integration after intense experiences is essential. This may include reflecting on insights gained, processing emotions, and finding ways to incorporate newfound knowledge into daily life.

---

4. When to Seek Professional Help

While many experiences during Kundalini awakening can be navigated through self-care and support, certain symptoms may require professional assistance:

- **Severe Mental Health Concerns:** If intense anxiety, panic, or confusion becomes overwhelming and interferes with daily functioning, seeking help from a qualified mental health professional is crucial.
- **Physical Health Issues:** If physical symptoms persist or worsen, it's essential to consult with a healthcare provider to rule out any underlying medical conditions.
- **Guidance from Experienced Practitioners:** Connecting with spiritual teachers or practitioners familiar with Kundalini awakening can provide valuable insights and support during challenging times.

Kundalini awakening can bring about intense challenges that may feel overwhelming. However, by understanding these challenges as opportunities for growth and healing, individuals can navigate the process with greater resilience and awareness. Embracing the journey of awakening, including its crises and spiritual purges, can ultimately lead to profound transformation and a deeper connection to one's true self.

Kundalini and the Nervous System – The Science Behind Energetic Activation

Kundalini awakening is often described in spiritual and esoteric terms, but recent advances in neuroscience and psychology have begun to shed light on the physiological processes involved. Understanding how **Kundalini energy** interacts with the **nervous system** can provide insights into the experiences associated with this powerful spiritual awakening.

1. Understanding Kundalini Energy

Kundalini is often depicted as a dormant, coiled serpent energy located at the base of the spine, within the **Muladhara (Root) chakra**. When awakened, this energy rises through the **Sushumna Nadi**, the central energy channel, activating the **chakras** and facilitating a transformative spiritual experience. The awakening of Kundalini is often accompanied by a range of **physical, emotional, and spiritual symptoms** that can be understood through the lens of neuroscience and the functioning of the nervous system.

2. The Nervous System and Its Role in Kundalini Awakening

The nervous system is a complex network that plays a crucial role in how we perceive and interact with the world around us. It is divided into two main parts:

A. Central Nervous System (CNS)

- **Brain and Spinal Cord:** The CNS processes information and coordinates responses, serving as the control center for bodily functions, including perception, movement, and thought.
- **Neuroplasticity:** The brain's ability to adapt and reorganize itself in response to experiences is fundamental to the transformational aspect of Kundalini awakening. Neuroplasticity allows for new neural connections and pathways to be formed, supporting changes in perception and consciousness.

B. Peripheral Nervous System (PNS)

- **Autonomic Nervous System (ANS):** The ANS regulates involuntary bodily functions, including heart rate, digestion, and respiration. It consists of two branches:
  - **Sympathetic Nervous System:** Responsible for the "fight or flight" response, which prepares the body for action in response to perceived threats.
  - **Parasympathetic Nervous System:** Known as the "rest and digest" system, it promotes relaxation, recovery, and energy conservation.

The interaction between the sympathetic and parasympathetic systems is crucial during Kundalini awakening, influencing how the body responds to the energy activation.

---

3. Energetic Activation and Its Effects on the Nervous System

A. Activation of the Sympathetic Nervous System

- **Heightened Awareness:** As Kundalini energy rises, it can trigger a sympathetic response, resulting in increased heart rate, heightened awareness, and intensified emotions. This state may feel exhilarating but can also lead to feelings of anxiety or panic as the body prepares for change.
- **Energy Surges:** Many individuals report experiencing bursts of energy or spontaneous movements (kriyas) as the Kundalini energy activates. This is similar to the body's natural responses during stress or excitement, where the sympathetic system is engaged.

B. Transition to the Parasympathetic Nervous System

- **Relaxation and Integration:** Following the initial surge of energy, the body may transition into a parasympathetic state, allowing for relaxation and integration of the experiences. This shift is essential for processing emotions and facilitating healing.
- **Restorative Processes:** Activation of the parasympathetic system promotes restorative processes, including improved digestion, lower heart rate, and a sense of calm. This state is conducive to deep meditation, reflection, and spiritual growth.

C. Neurotransmitter and Hormonal Changes

- **Dopamine and Serotonin:** Awakening experiences can lead to changes in neurotransmitter levels, including increased dopamine and serotonin, which can enhance mood, promote feelings of joy, and support emotional well-being.

- **Cortisol and Stress Response:** The initial stages of Kundalini rising may cause elevated cortisol levels (the stress hormone), which can contribute to feelings of anxiety or tension. Learning to manage stress through grounding techniques can help regulate these levels.

4. Chakras and the Nervous System

A. Chakra System and Energy Flow

The chakra system consists of **seven primary energy centers** aligned along the spine, each associated with different aspects of consciousness and physiological functions. When Kundalini energy rises, it activates these chakras, influencing the nervous system in various ways:

- **Root Chakra (Muladhara):** Grounding and survival instincts; activation can stabilize the nervous system.
- **Sacral Chakra (Svadhisthana):** Creativity and emotions; related to the autonomic nervous system's regulation of pleasure and reproduction.
- **Solar Plexus Chakra (Manipura):** Personal power and confidence; activation can influence the sympathetic nervous system, heightening self-esteem and motivation.
- **Heart Chakra (Anahata):** Love and compassion; promotes emotional balance and strengthens the parasympathetic response.
- **Throat Chakra (Vishuddha):** Communication and expression; fosters clarity and reduces anxiety in self-expression.
- **Third Eye Chakra (Ajna):** Intuition and perception; enhances awareness and mental clarity, allowing for deeper understanding.
- **Crown Chakra (Sahasrara):** Spiritual connection and enlightenment; fosters a sense of oneness, promoting a calming effect on the nervous system.

B. Energetic Blockages

- **Dysfunction and Discomfort:** Blockages in the chakra system can lead to physical or emotional discomfort, which may manifest as symptoms during Kundalini awakening. Understanding these blockages can guide individuals in their healing process.
- **Healing and Realignment:** Engaging in practices like yoga, meditation, and energy healing can facilitate the release of blockages, promoting balanced energy flow and supporting overall nervous system health.

5. Practical Approaches to Support the Nervous System During Kundalini Awakening

A. Grounding Techniques

- **Mindfulness Practices:** Engaging in mindfulness and meditation can help individuals remain present and calm during intense energy shifts.
- **Nature Connection:** Spending time outdoors and grounding oneself in nature can stabilize energy and promote a sense of safety.

B. Breathwork and Relaxation

- **Pranayama:** Breath control techniques can balance the autonomic nervous system, enhancing relaxation and facilitating energy flow.
- **Progressive Muscle Relaxation:** This technique can help release tension and calm the nervous system, allowing for deeper integration of experiences.

C. Healthy Lifestyle Choices

- **Balanced Diet:** Consuming a nourishing diet can support the body's energy levels and overall well-being.
- **Regular Exercise:** Physical activity promotes circulation and helps release pent-up energy, contributing to emotional and physical balance.

D. Seek Professional Guidance

- **Therapeutic Support:** Consulting with therapists or practitioners knowledgeable in energy work can provide support during challenging experiences associated with Kundalini awakening.
- **Energy Healing Modalities:** Practices such as Reiki, acupuncture, or chakra healing can help facilitate energy flow and promote balance in the nervous system.

Understanding the relationship between **Kundalini energy** and the **nervous system** can help individuals navigate the complexities of awakening with greater awareness. By recognizing the physiological processes at play and employing grounding techniques, individuals can foster resilience and facilitate healing during this transformative journey. Embracing the challenges and insights gained from Kundalini awakening ultimately leads to personal growth, spiritual insight, and a deeper connection to oneself and the universe.

Part III: Shakti's Path to Awakening

Sacred Feminine Practices – Rituals, Mantras, and Meditations to Invoke Shakti

The **Sacred Feminine**, often represented as **Shakti**, embodies divine feminine energy, creativity, intuition, and the nurturing aspects of life. Engaging in practices that honor and invoke Shakti can deepen one's connection to this powerful energy, facilitating personal transformation and spiritual growth. Here, we'll explore various practices, including rituals, mantras, and meditations that can help individuals connect with the Sacred Feminine.

---

1. Understanding Shakti

Shakti is the dynamic, creative energy that powers the universe, often personified through various goddesses in Hindu mythology, such as **Durga**, **Kali**, **Lakshmi**, and **Saraswati**. Engaging with Shakti allows individuals to harness their own creative potential, intuitive wisdom, and transformative power. Sacred Feminine practices aim to invoke this energy, promoting healing, empowerment, and spiritual awakening.

---

2. Rituals to Invoke Shakti

Rituals are powerful tools for creating sacred space and inviting divine energy into one's life. Here are some practices that can help invoke Shakti:

A. Creating a Sacred Space

- **Altar Setup:** Designate a space in your home to create an altar. Include images or statues of goddesses, candles, flowers, crystals, and other meaningful objects that resonate with your intention to connect with the Sacred Feminine.
- **Cleansing the Space:** Use sage, palo santo, or incense to cleanse the area, setting the intention to invite Shakti into the space.

B. Offering Rituals

- **Food Offerings (Naivedya):** Prepare a simple meal or sweet treat and offer it to the divine feminine as a gesture of gratitude. This can be done during a specific festival or on days dedicated to goddess worship.
- **Flower Offerings:** Create a garland of flowers or place fresh flowers at your altar as a symbol of beauty and devotion. Flowers represent purity and can attract positive energy.

C. Full Moon Rituals

- **Lunar Connection:** The full moon is often associated with the feminine and is an excellent time to perform rituals. Light candles, meditate, and set intentions for the month ahead. Reflect on your emotional landscape and release what no longer serves you.
- **Dance and Movement:** Engage in a dance or movement practice under the full moon, allowing your body to express the energy of Shakti. This can be a liberating and joyful way to connect with the divine feminine.

D. Celebration of Goddess Festivals

- **Navaratri:** Participate in the nine nights of worship dedicated to the goddess Durga. Each night is associated with a different form of the goddess, allowing for diverse expressions of Shakti.
- **Dussehra or Diwali:** Celebrate these festivals that honor the victory of light over darkness and the triumph of divine feminine energy. Engage in prayers, offerings, and communal gatherings.

---

3. Mantras to Invoke Shakti

Mantras are sacred sounds or phrases that can elevate consciousness and connect individuals with divine energies. Here are some powerful mantras associated with the Sacred Feminine:

**A. Om Shakti Namah

- **Meaning:** This mantra translates to "Salutations to the Divine Energy." Reciting it invokes the energy of Shakti, promoting empowerment and transformation.

**B. Maha Kali Mantra

- **"Om Krim Kalikayai Namah":** This mantra honors Kali, the fierce form of the goddess, associated with transformation, strength, and liberation from fear. Chanting this mantra can help release attachments and invite courage.

**C. Saraswati Vandana

- **"Om Saraswati Namah":** This mantra pays homage to Saraswati, the goddess of knowledge, arts, and wisdom. Reciting it can enhance creativity and clarity of thought.

**D. Lakshmi Mantra

- **"Om Shreem Mahalakshmiyei Namah":** This mantra invokes Lakshmi, the goddess of abundance and prosperity. Chanting it can attract wealth, prosperity, and well-being into one's life.

**E. Durga Gayatri Mantra

- **"Om Dharmarajaya Vidmahe, Maa Durgaaya Dhimahi, Tanno Durga Prachodayat":** This powerful Gayatri mantra calls upon the protective and nurturing aspects of Durga. Reciting it can invoke strength and resilience during challenging times.

---

4. Meditations to Connect with Shakti

Meditation is a powerful practice for connecting with the Sacred Feminine and inviting Shakti into one's life. Here are some meditative practices to consider:

A. Kundalini Awakening Meditation

- **Sitting in a Comfortable Position:** Begin by sitting comfortably with a straight spine. Close your eyes and take several deep breaths.
- **Focus on the Base of the Spine:** Visualize a warm, coiled energy at the base of your spine (Muladhara chakra). Imagine it slowly rising as you inhale, moving through each chakra.
- **Chanting Mantras:** As you visualize this energy rising, chant a mantra (e.g., **"Om Shakti Namah"**) to enhance the connection with Shakti.

B. Guided Visualization

- **Visualize Divine Feminine Energy:** Close your eyes and visualize a radiant feminine figure representing Shakti. Feel her presence enveloping you in warmth and love.
- **Inviting Qualities:** Invite qualities such as creativity, intuition, and empowerment into your being. Allow yourself to receive the energy and guidance from the Divine Feminine.

C. Heart-Centered Meditation

- **Focusing on the Heart Chakra:** Sit comfortably and bring your awareness to your heart center (Anahata chakra). Feel the warmth and love radiating from this center.
- **Breathing into the Heart:** Inhale deeply and imagine filling your heart with light and love. As you exhale, release any blockages or fears, allowing your heart to open to the energy of Shakti.

D. Dance Meditation

- **Embodied Movement:** Engage in free-form dance, allowing your body to move intuitively. As you dance, feel the energy of Shakti flowing through you.

- **Express Your Emotions:** Let go of inhibitions and express your emotions through movement, connecting deeply with your body and the divine feminine energy within.

5. Incorporating Sacred Feminine Practices into Daily Life

A. Mindful Living

- **Daily Rituals:** Incorporate small rituals into your daily routine, such as lighting a candle, offering gratitude, or dedicating time for reflection and intention-setting.
- **Nurturing Self-Care:** Prioritize self-care practices that honor your feminine energy, such as nourishing meals, relaxation, and creative expression.

B. Community and Connection

- **Join Women's Circles:** Participate in women's circles or groups that celebrate the Sacred Feminine. Sharing experiences and supporting one another can deepen your connection to Shakti.
- **Collaborative Rituals:** Engage in collaborative rituals with friends or community members to amplify the energy of the Sacred Feminine.

C. Creativity and Expression

- **Artistic Practices:** Engage in creative pursuits such as painting, writing, or crafting. Allow your creative energy to flow and express the essence of Shakti through your art.
- **Dance and Movement Classes:** Explore dance or movement classes that emphasize feminine expression, such as belly dance, sacred dance, or ecstatic dance.

Engaging in sacred feminine practices allows individuals to connect with the transformative energy of Shakti, fostering personal growth, empowerment, and spiritual awakening. By incorporating rituals, mantras, and meditations into daily life, one can cultivate a deeper relationship with the Sacred Feminine and embrace the divine qualities within. These practices not only honor the feminine energy but also encourage individuals to express their authentic selves and embrace their unique paths.

Shakti and the Breath – Pranayama Techniques for Activating Kundalini

Breath is often referred to as the bridge between the physical and spiritual realms, playing a pivotal role in many spiritual practices, particularly in the context of **Kundalini awakening**. **Pranayama**, the ancient practice of breath control in yoga, is essential for harnessing and activating **Shakti**, the divine feminine energy. This detailed exploration will cover the relationship between breath and Shakti, how pranayama techniques can activate Kundalini, and practical guidance on incorporating these practices into your spiritual journey.

1. Understanding the Relationship Between Breath and Shakti

A. The Nature of Shakti

Shakti represents the dynamic, creative force that drives all life and transformation. In the context of Kundalini, Shakti is often depicted as a coiled serpent energy residing at the base of the spine. When awakened, this energy rises through the chakras, leading to profound spiritual experiences and heightened consciousness.

B. Breath as Life Force

Breath (or **prana**) is considered the vital life force that sustains all living beings. In yogic philosophy, breath is synonymous with **Shakti**, as it energizes the body and mind. By consciously controlling the breath through pranayama techniques, practitioners can tap into this vital energy, facilitating the awakening and movement of Kundalini energy within.

C. Pranayama and the Nervous System

Pranayama techniques impact the **nervous system**, promoting relaxation, balance, and heightened awareness. By regulating breath, practitioners can activate the parasympathetic nervous system, reducing stress and creating an optimal state for Kundalini awakening.

2. Pranayama Techniques for Activating Kundalini

Here are several pranayama techniques that can help activate Shakti and facilitate Kundalini awakening:

A. Nadi Shodhana (Alternate Nostril Breathing)

Purpose: This technique purifies the energy channels (nadis) and balances the flow of prana between the left and right hemispheres of the brain.

- **How to Practice:**
    1. Sit comfortably in a meditative posture with a straight spine.
    2. Use your right thumb to close your right nostril.
    3. Inhale deeply through your left nostril for a count of four.

4. Close the left nostril with your ring finger and release the right nostril. Exhale through the right nostril for a count of four.
5. Inhale through the right nostril for a count of four.
6. Close the right nostril, open the left, and exhale for a count of four.
7. Repeat this cycle for 5–10 minutes, focusing on the breath and visualizing energy flowing through the nadis.

B. Kapalabhati (Skull Shining Breath)

Purpose: This energizing technique clears stagnant energy, enhances focus, and activates the solar plexus chakra, promoting a sense of vitality and awakening Shakti.

- **How to Practice:**
    1. Sit in a comfortable position with a straight spine.
    2. Take a deep breath in through the nose, filling your lungs completely.
    3. Exhale forcefully through the nose while contracting the abdominal muscles.
    4. Allow the inhalation to happen passively and naturally between each forceful exhalation.
    5. Continue this cycle for 30 seconds to 1 minute, gradually increasing the duration as you become more comfortable with the practice.

C. Bhastrika (Bellows Breath)

Purpose: This vigorous technique increases energy levels, warms the body, and prepares the practitioner for deeper states of meditation, enhancing the awakening of Kundalini.

- **How to Practice:**
    1. Sit in a comfortable position with your spine straight.
    2. Inhale deeply through the nose while expanding your belly and chest.
    3. Exhale forcefully through the nose, contracting the abdomen.
    4. Perform this for 10 rapid breaths, followed by a slow, deep inhalation.
    5. Hold the breath for a few seconds before exhaling slowly.
    6. Repeat this cycle for 3–5 minutes, focusing on the rhythm of your breath and the energy it generates.

D. Ujjayi Breath (Victorious Breath)

Purpose: This calming technique creates internal heat, promotes concentration, and connects the practitioner to their inner power, facilitating the flow of Shakti.

- **How to Practice:**
    1. Sit comfortably or lie down in a relaxed position.
    2. Inhale deeply through the nose, slightly constricting the back of the throat to create a soft, whispering sound.
    3. Exhale through the nose, maintaining the throat constriction to create the same sound.
    4. Continue for several minutes, focusing on the sound of your breath and the sensations it creates in your body.

E. Siddhi Pranayama (Energizing Breath)

Purpose: This technique is designed to directly activate Kundalini energy by increasing energy flow through the body.

- **How to Practice:**
    1. Sit in a comfortable position with a straight spine.
    2. Take a deep inhalation while visualizing Shakti rising from the base of your spine.
    3. Hold the breath for a few seconds while focusing on the energy movement within.
    4. Exhale deeply while visualizing the energy flowing upward through each chakra.
    5. Repeat this for several cycles, gradually increasing the duration of inhalation and retention.

---

3. Tips for Effective Pranayama Practice

A. Set Your Intention

Before beginning your pranayama practice, set a clear intention for what you wish to achieve, whether it is to awaken Kundalini, cultivate inner peace, or enhance your connection to Shakti.

B. Create a Sacred Space

Designate a quiet, comfortable space for your practice, free from distractions. Light candles or incense to create an atmosphere conducive to meditation and focus.

C. Practice Regularly

Consistency is key to experiencing the benefits of pranayama. Incorporate these techniques into your daily routine, even if only for a few minutes, to build a deeper connection with Shakti.

D. Listen to Your Body

Be mindful of your body's signals during practice. If you experience discomfort, dizziness, or anxiety, return to a natural breathing pattern and take a break. Pranayama should feel energizing and nurturing, not overwhelming.

E. Combine with Meditation

After completing your pranayama practice, transition into meditation. This can help you integrate the energy generated through breathwork and deepen your connection with Shakti.

Pranayama techniques provide powerful tools for activating Kundalini and connecting with the Sacred Feminine energy of Shakti. By consciously harnessing the breath, practitioners can facilitate the flow of energy within the body, leading to personal transformation, spiritual awakening, and heightened awareness. Incorporating these practices into your spiritual journey can deepen your understanding of the divine feminine and empower you to embrace your authentic self.

Mantras and Sounds of Awakening – Vibrations that Align with the Divine Feminine

Mantras and sound play a crucial role in spiritual practices, especially when it comes to awakening and connecting with the **Divine Feminine**, often represented by the energy of **Shakti**. The vibrational quality of sound can profoundly impact the mind, body, and spirit, facilitating healing, transformation, and spiritual growth. This exploration will delve into the significance of mantras, specific sounds associated with the Divine Feminine, and practical guidance on how to use these vibrational tools for awakening.

---

1. Understanding the Power of Sound and Vibration

A. The Science of Sound

Sound is a form of energy that travels in waves, and everything in the universe vibrates at a certain frequency. The **frequency** of sound can influence our emotional, mental, and physical states. In many spiritual traditions, sound is seen as a primary vehicle for manifesting intentions and connecting with higher consciousness.

B. Mantras and Their Purpose

Mantras are sacred sounds, syllables, or phrases that hold spiritual significance. In Sanskrit, the word "mantra" can be translated to mean "that which protects the mind." They are used to focus the mind, invoke specific energies, and align oneself with the desired frequency of consciousness. When repeated, mantras can create powerful vibrations that resonate with the Divine Feminine and facilitate spiritual awakening.

2. Mantras Associated with the Divine Feminine

Here are some key mantras that embody the energy of the Divine Feminine and can be used for spiritual awakening:

A. Om

- **Significance:** Considered the primordial sound, "Om" represents the essence of the universe and the ultimate reality. It embodies the sacredness of creation and the interconnectedness of all beings.
- **Practice:** Chanting "Om" creates a profound sense of peace and alignment with the Divine. It can be used at the beginning and end of any mantra practice to establish sacred space.

B. Om Shakti Namah

- **Meaning:** "Salutations to the Divine Energy."
- **Purpose:** This mantra honors Shakti, the goddess energy that represents the divine feminine creative force. It can be chanted to invoke empowerment, creativity, and transformation.
- **Practice:** Recite this mantra during meditation or while visualizing the flow of Shakti energy within your body.

C. Maha Kali Mantra

- **"Om Krim Kalikayai Namah":**
- **Significance:** This mantra invokes Kali, the fierce aspect of the goddess who embodies transformation, protection, and liberation from fear.
- **Purpose:** It can be chanted to release attachments and invoke courage in times of challenge.
- **Practice:** Repeat this mantra during rituals or when seeking strength and resilience in overcoming obstacles.

D. Lakshmi Mantra

- **"Om Shreem Mahalakshmiyei Namah":**

- **Significance:** This mantra honors Lakshmi, the goddess of abundance, prosperity, and well-being.
- **Purpose:** Chanting this mantra can attract abundance and positive energy into one's life.
- **Practice:** Use this mantra during meditation or visualization of your goals, inviting prosperity into your reality.

E. Saraswati Vandana

- **"Om Saraswati Namah":**
- **Significance:** This mantra pays homage to Saraswati, the goddess of knowledge, wisdom, and creativity.
- **Purpose:** It enhances clarity of thought and creative expression.
- **Practice:** Chant this mantra before engaging in creative pursuits or while studying to invite focus and inspiration.

F. Durga Gayatri Mantra

- **"Om Dharmarajaya Vidmahe, Maa Durgaaya Dhimahi, Tanno Durga Prachodayat":**
- **Significance:** This powerful Gayatri mantra honors Durga, the protective and nurturing aspect of the Divine Feminine.
- **Purpose:** It invokes strength, protection, and empowerment.
- **Practice:** Use this mantra in meditation, particularly when facing challenges or seeking guidance.

---

3. The Role of Sound Healing in Spiritual Awakening

A. Sound Healing Techniques

Sound healing utilizes various instruments and techniques to facilitate healing and awakening. Here are some common practices that can be used alongside mantra chanting:

1. Singing Bowls

- **Description:** Tibetan singing bowls produce rich, resonant tones that create a calming atmosphere and can be used to balance energy.
- **Practice:** Use a singing bowl while chanting mantras, allowing the vibrations to amplify the intention and connect with the energy of the Divine Feminine.

2. Tuning Forks

- **Description:** Tuning forks emit specific frequencies that can help align the energy centers in the body.
- **Practice:** Strike a tuning fork and place it near the body while chanting mantras to enhance the vibrational effects.

3. Drumming

- **Description:** Rhythmic drumming can induce altered states of consciousness, connecting individuals to the earth and the divine.
- **Practice:** Use drumming in conjunction with mantra chanting to create a powerful energetic field that aligns with the Divine Feminine.

---

4. How to Practice Mantras and Sound for Awakening

A. Setting the Intention

Before beginning your practice, set a clear intention for what you wish to achieve. Whether you seek empowerment, healing, or connection with the Divine Feminine, articulating your intention can enhance the effectiveness of your practice.

B. Creating a Sacred Space

Designate a quiet and comfortable space for your practice. Light candles, burn incense, or use essential oils to create an environment that resonates with your intention.

C. Practicing with Presence

- **Begin with Breath:** Start by taking a few deep breaths to center yourself and connect with your body.
- **Chant Aloud or Silently:** Choose a mantra that resonates with you and chant it aloud or silently, focusing on the vibration and meaning of the sound.
- **Focus on the Heart Center:** As you chant, bring your awareness to your heart center (Anahata chakra), allowing the sound to resonate within you and amplify your connection to the Divine Feminine.

D. Length and Frequency of Practice

- **Regular Practice:** Aim to practice regularly, even if only for a few minutes each day. Consistency can deepen your connection with the Divine Feminine energy.
- **Longer Sessions:** For more profound experiences, dedicate longer sessions (15-30 minutes) to mantra chanting, integrating sound healing techniques as needed.

E. Reflect and Integrate

For our free video kundalini training visit https://shiftnetwork.infusionsoft.com/go/akeg/a20331

After your practice, take a few moments to reflect on your experience. Journal any insights or feelings that arose during the session, and consider how you can integrate these into your daily life.

The use of mantras and sound offers a powerful pathway for awakening the Divine Feminine within us. Through the vibrational quality of sound, practitioners can connect deeply with Shakti, facilitating personal transformation, healing, and spiritual growth. By incorporating mantra chanting and sound healing techniques into your spiritual practice, you can cultivate a profound relationship with the Divine Feminine and awaken your innate power.

Mudras and Sacred Gestures – Activating Shakti Through the Body

Mudras, often referred to as sacred gestures or hand positions, play a significant role in many spiritual and healing traditions, particularly within **yoga** and **Tantra**. These gestures can activate **Shakti**, the divine feminine energy, and facilitate the flow of **prana** (life force energy) throughout the body. By using mudras, practitioners can enhance their meditation, deepen their spiritual practices, and connect more profoundly with the energy of the Divine Feminine. This discussion will explore the importance of mudras, specific mudras associated with Shakti, and practical guidance on how to incorporate them into your spiritual practice.

---

1. Understanding the Power of Mudras

A. Definition and Significance

Mudras are symbolic hand gestures that have been used for centuries in various spiritual traditions, particularly in **Hinduism**, **Buddhism**, and **yoga**. The word "mudra" is derived from Sanskrit, meaning "seal" or "mark." Each mudra serves as a means of channeling energy and can have profound effects on the mind, body, and spirit.

B. The Connection to Energy

Mudras are believed to influence the flow of energy within the body, specifically in relation to the **chakras** and **nadis** (energy channels). By creating specific hand shapes and gestures, practitioners can activate or balance the energy associated with these energy centers, facilitating spiritual awakening and connection to Shakti.

C. The Science Behind Mudras

Research has shown that mudras can influence neurological and physiological processes in the body. The specific positioning of the hands can stimulate nerve endings and meridians, promoting relaxation, focus, and healing. Mudras can also enhance meditative states, making them an effective tool for spiritual practice.

2. Mudras to Activate Shakti

Here are several mudras that are particularly effective for activating Shakti and connecting with the Divine Feminine:

A. Anjali Mudra (Prayer Gesture)

- **Description:** In this mudra, the palms are brought together in front of the heart center (Anahata chakra), fingers pointing upward.
- **Significance:** Anjali Mudra symbolizes respect, gratitude, and the union of masculine and feminine energies. It invites a sense of peace and connection with the Divine.
- **Practice:** Use this mudra during meditation or prayer to center yourself and cultivate an attitude of reverence and openness to Shakti.

B. Hakini Mudra

- **Description:** In Hakini Mudra, the fingertips of both hands touch each other, forming a dome shape above the head.
- **Significance:** This mudra enhances concentration, mental clarity, and balance, facilitating the activation of higher consciousness and spiritual insight.
- **Practice:** Hold this mudra while meditating, focusing on drawing energy into your mind and connecting with Shakti's wisdom.

C. Shakti Mudra

- **Description:** To perform Shakti Mudra, fold the ring and little fingers into the palm while extending the other fingers.
- **Significance:** This mudra is specifically dedicated to activating Shakti energy, encouraging creativity and self-expression.
- **Practice:** Use this mudra during creative practices, such as writing or painting, to invite inspiration and energize your creative flow.

D. Gyan Mudra (Knowledge Gesture)

- **Description:** In Gyan Mudra, the tip of the thumb touches the tip of the index finger, while the other three fingers remain extended.
- **Significance:** This mudra is associated with wisdom, knowledge, and spiritual awakening. It opens the channels of communication with the divine and enhances intuition.

- **Practice:** Incorporate Gyan Mudra into your meditation or study sessions to deepen your connection with knowledge and insight from the Divine Feminine.

E. Dhyana Mudra (Meditation Gesture)

- **Description:** In Dhyana Mudra, the hands are placed in the lap, with the palms facing up and one hand resting on top of the other, fingers extended.
- **Significance:** This mudra promotes inner peace and calmness, creating a receptive state for meditation and allowing the practitioner to connect deeply with Shakti.
- **Practice:** Use Dhyana Mudra during meditation to cultivate a sense of stillness and openness to receiving divine energy.

F. Ujjayi Mudra

- **Description:** This mudra is performed by slightly constricting the throat and creating a soft sound as you breathe.
- **Significance:** It enhances prana flow and activates the throat chakra (Vishuddha), facilitating the expression of your truth and creativity.
- **Practice:** Combine Ujjayi Mudra with deep breathing exercises to deepen your connection to Shakti and enhance your vocal expression.

---

3. How to Practice Mudras Effectively

A. Set Your Intention

Before engaging in mudra practice, set a clear intention for what you wish to achieve. Whether it's to connect with Shakti, enhance creativity, or promote healing, having a focused intention can amplify the effectiveness of your practice.

B. Create a Sacred Space

Find a quiet, comfortable place to practice mudras. Light candles, use incense, or play soft music to create an inviting atmosphere that resonates with the energy of the Divine Feminine.

C. Combine with Breath and Meditation

- **Focus on Breath:** Begin by taking a few deep breaths to center yourself and create a state of relaxation.
- **Hold the Mudra:** Once you're centered, adopt your chosen mudra while continuing to breathe deeply. Visualize energy flowing through your body and into your chosen mudra.

- **Meditate:** Allow yourself to remain in this position for several minutes, focusing on your intention and the sensations that arise.

D. Length of Practice

Start with short sessions (5–10 minutes) and gradually increase the duration as you become more comfortable with the practice. Consistency is essential, so aim to incorporate mudras into your daily routine.

E. Integrate with Movement

Mudras can also be incorporated into yoga practice. Use them during asanas to enhance your connection to Shakti and deepen your practice. For example, holding Anjali Mudra at the heart center during standing poses can cultivate a sense of grounding and connection.

Mudras and sacred gestures provide a powerful means of activating Shakti and connecting with the Divine Feminine. By using these hand positions, practitioners can channel energy, enhance spiritual practices, and cultivate a deeper connection to their inner power. Incorporating mudras into your daily routine can facilitate personal transformation, spiritual growth, and a profound relationship with the sacred energy of Shakti.

The Role of Dance and Movement – Expressing and Channeling Kundalini Energy

Dance and movement have long been recognized as powerful forms of expression and channels for spiritual energy across various cultures and spiritual traditions. When it comes to **Kundalini energy**, which represents the primal life force lying dormant at the base of the spine, movement and dance can serve as potent vehicles for its awakening and expression. This discussion will explore the connection between dance, movement, and Kundalini energy, the different forms of movement that facilitate this energy's flow, and practical ways to incorporate dance into spiritual practice.

---

1. Understanding Kundalini Energy

A. Definition of Kundalini

Kundalini is often described as a coiled serpent that resides at the base of the spine (Muladhara chakra). When awakened, this energy ascends through the chakras, leading to heightened awareness, spiritual growth, and profound transformation. The process of Kundalini awakening can be both exhilarating and challenging, as it may bring forth buried emotions, insights, and energies that require integration.

B. The Role of Movement in Awakening

Movement plays a vital role in the process of Kundalini awakening. Through physical expression, individuals can release stagnant energy, emotional blockages, and tension within the body, creating a more conducive environment for the rise of Kundalini energy. Dance and movement also allow for the embodiment of spiritual experiences, facilitating deeper connections to the self and the divine.

2. Forms of Dance and Movement that Channel Kundalini Energy

A. Sacred Dance Traditions

Various cultures have utilized dance as a means of spiritual expression and connection to the divine. Some notable sacred dance traditions that align with the expression of Kundalini energy include:

1. Sufi Whirling

- **Description:** Practiced by Sufi mystics, whirling involves spinning in repetitive circles to enter an altered state of consciousness.
- **Connection to Kundalini:** The movement helps to release pent-up energy, allowing practitioners to experience a deep connection to divine love and unity.

2. Bharatanatyam and Classical Indian Dance

- **Description:** These traditional dance forms emphasize intricate hand gestures (mudras), facial expressions (abhinaya), and rhythmic footwork.
- **Connection to Kundalini:** The choreography often embodies spiritual themes and stories from Hindu mythology, facilitating the flow of Kundalini energy through the dancer's body and expressing divine feminine qualities.

3. African Dance

- **Description:** African dance is characterized by dynamic movements that connect the dancer to the earth, ancestors, and community.
- **Connection to Kundalini:** The emphasis on rhythmic body movement and connection to the ground allows for the free flow of energy, facilitating the awakening of Kundalini.

B. Freeform and Ecstatic Dance

- **Description:** Freeform or ecstatic dance involves spontaneous movement without structured choreography. Participants allow their bodies to express themselves freely to music.
- **Connection to Kundalini:** This form of dance encourages the release of inhibitions and emotional expression, allowing Kundalini energy to rise and flow through the body without restraint.

C. Yoga and Movement Practices

1. Kundalini Yoga

- **Description:** Kundalini Yoga combines physical postures, breathwork, chanting, and meditation to awaken Kundalini energy.
- **Connection to Movement:** The dynamic movements and specific sequences are designed to activate energy centers (chakras) and facilitate the rise of Kundalini.

2. Vinyasa and Flow Yoga

- **Description:** These styles of yoga emphasize continuous movement and breath synchronization, creating a dynamic flow of energy.
- **Connection to Kundalini:** The fluid movements promote the circulation of prana, helping to awaken and channel Kundalini energy throughout the body.

---

3. The Psychological and Emotional Aspects of Dance

A. Expressing Emotions through Movement

Dance serves as a powerful outlet for emotional expression, allowing individuals to process and release pent-up feelings. As Kundalini energy rises, it may bring unresolved emotions to the surface. Engaging in dance can help to integrate these emotions, facilitating healing and growth.

B. Creating a Mind-Body Connection

Movement and dance cultivate a heightened awareness of the body and its sensations. This connection is essential for the process of Kundalini awakening, as it allows individuals to tune in to their physical, emotional, and energetic states.

C. Expanding Consciousness

Engaging in ecstatic or freeform dance can lead to altered states of consciousness, promoting feelings of bliss, unity, and connection with the divine. These experiences can enhance spiritual insight and understanding, facilitating a deeper connection with Kundalini energy.

---

4. Practical Ways to Incorporate Dance into Kundalini Practice

A. Setting Intentions

Before engaging in dance, set clear intentions for your practice. Whether it's to connect with your inner self, release emotional blockages, or awaken Kundalini energy, having a focused intention can enhance the effectiveness of your dance practice.

B. Creating a Sacred Space

Designate a comfortable and safe space for your dance practice. Clear the area of distractions, and consider using candles, incense, or uplifting music to create an inviting atmosphere.

C. Warm-Up and Breathwork

Begin your practice with gentle warm-up exercises and breathwork to connect with your body and prepare for movement. Breathing exercises such as **Pranayama** can help facilitate the flow of prana and energize the body.

D. Allow for Spontaneity

Engage in spontaneous movement without judgment or expectation. Allow your body to express itself freely, following the rhythm of the music or your breath. Embrace whatever arises—whether it's joy, sadness, or energy—as part of your practice.

E. Use Guided Movement Practices

Consider participating in guided movement practices, such as **Kundalini Yoga classes**, ecstatic dance sessions, or workshops focused on movement and spiritual expression. These environments can provide valuable support and encouragement.

F. Reflect and Integrate

After your dance session, take some time to reflect on your experience. Journal about any insights, emotions, or sensations that arose during the practice. Consider how you can integrate these experiences into your daily life.

Dance and movement offer powerful avenues for expressing and channeling Kundalini energy. By engaging in sacred dance traditions, freeform movement, or yoga practices, individuals can awaken and embody the divine energy of Shakti within themselves. The process of moving the body not only facilitates the release of emotional and energetic blockages but also enhances spiritual awareness and connection.

Tantric Practices for Shakti Activation – Exploring Sacred Sexuality and Energy Exchange

Tantra, an ancient spiritual tradition originating from India, encompasses a wide range of practices aimed at achieving union with the divine, personal transformation, and the awakening of latent energies, particularly **Shakti**, the divine feminine force. Within the context of Tantra, sacred sexuality plays a crucial role, as it recognizes the profound connection between sexual energy, spirituality, and the awakening of Kundalini. This discussion will delve into the key elements of Tantric practices for Shakti activation, including the philosophy of sacred sexuality, various techniques for energy exchange, and the significance of creating a sacred space for these practices.

1. Understanding Tantric Philosophy and Sacred Sexuality

A. Definition of Tantra

Tantra is a complex spiritual system that integrates philosophy, rituals, meditation, and physical practices. It seeks to awaken higher states of consciousness by harmonizing the dual forces of **Shiva** (masculine energy) and **Shakti** (feminine energy). In this context, sexuality is viewed as a sacred and powerful force that can lead to spiritual enlightenment when approached with reverence and intention.

B. The Role of Sacred Sexuality

Sacred sexuality in Tantra transcends mere physical pleasure; it is about experiencing profound connection, intimacy, and unity with oneself and one's partner. This form of sexuality acknowledges the energetic dimensions of intimacy, allowing practitioners to harness sexual energy (often called **Kundalini** or **sexual energy**) for spiritual growth and Shakti activation.

C. The Union of Shiva and Shakti

In Tantric philosophy, the union of Shiva and Shakti symbolizes the merging of consciousness (Shiva) and energy (Shakti). This union is not limited to physical intimacy but extends to all aspects of existence. By activating Shakti through sacred sexuality, individuals can awaken deeper spiritual insights and connections with the divine.

2. Key Tantric Practices for Shakti Activation

A. Breathwork (Pranayama)

- **Description:** Breath is considered a powerful tool for cultivating and circulating energy within the body. Tantric practitioners often use specific breathing techniques to awaken Kundalini and enhance sexual energy.
- **Techniques:**
  - **Ujjayi Breath:** This oceanic breath helps to calm the mind and increase prana flow.
  - **Alternate Nostril Breathing:** Balances the masculine and feminine energies and prepares the practitioner for deeper energy exchange.

B. Meditation and Visualization

- **Description:** Meditation is a foundational practice in Tantra. Practitioners can use visualization techniques to connect with Shakti and channel her energy.
- **Techniques:**
    - **Shakti Visualization:** Visualize Shakti as a vibrant energy at the base of the spine, envisioning her ascent through the chakras.
    - **Chakra Meditations:** Focus on each chakra, imagining it as a lotus flower opening and blooming, facilitating the flow of energy.

C. Sacred Touch and Sensuality

- **Description:** Tantric practices emphasize the importance of touch as a means of energy exchange. Sacred touch involves conscious, loving, and intentional physical contact between partners.
- **Practices:**
    - **Tantric Massage:** Aimed at awakening Kundalini and enhancing intimacy, Tantric massage incorporates slow, deliberate movements and breath synchronization to deepen the connection between partners.
    - **Caressing and Holding:** Engaging in mindful caresses, holding each other, and exploring the body with presence and awareness fosters deeper intimacy and connection.

D. Rituals and Ceremonies

- **Description:** Rituals create a sacred atmosphere that enhances the experience of Shakti activation. They often involve the use of symbols, offerings, and guided practices.
- **Examples:**
    - **Creating a Sacred Space:** Set up an altar with meaningful items (flowers, candles, crystals) to honor the divine.
    - **Invocation:** Begin with an invocation to the divine feminine, calling upon Shakti to guide and bless the practice.

E. Energy Exchange and Kundalini Awakening

- **Description:** Energy exchange between partners is a central theme in Tantric practices. By cultivating awareness of energy flow, partners can amplify their experiences and deepen their connection.
- **Practices:**
    - **Eye Gazing:** Engage in prolonged eye contact to create an intimate connection and facilitate energy transfer.

- **Circulating Energy:** In a partnered practice, visualize the energy flowing between partners, creating a continuous loop of energy exchange.

---

3. Creating a Sacred Space for Tantric Practices

A. Setting the Intention

Before engaging in Tantric practices, partners should discuss their intentions and desires. Establishing mutual goals helps to align energies and create a shared experience.

B. Preparing the Environment

Create a nurturing and sacred environment conducive to the practice. This may include dim lighting, soft music, candles, and comfortable bedding. Aromatherapy with essential oils can also enhance the sensory experience.

C. Establishing Boundaries and Communication

Clear communication and consent are essential in Tantric practices. Discuss boundaries, desires, and comfort levels to ensure a safe and respectful environment for both partners.

---

4. The Benefits of Tantric Practices for Shakti Activation

A. Spiritual Growth and Awakening

Tantric practices facilitate spiritual awakening and deeper self-awareness. By connecting with Shakti, individuals can access their inner wisdom and higher consciousness.

B. Enhanced Intimacy and Connection

Engaging in sacred sexuality fosters deeper emotional and physical intimacy between partners. This connection can strengthen relationships and promote a sense of unity.

C. Healing and Release

Tantric practices can help release emotional blockages and trauma, promoting healing and integration. The energy exchange and sacred touch can facilitate the processing of stored emotions, leading to profound transformation.

D. Empowerment and Creativity

By awakening Shakti, individuals tap into their creative potential and personal power. This empowerment can manifest in various aspects of life, including relationships, career, and personal expression.

Tantric practices offer a profound pathway for activating Shakti and harnessing the transformative power of sacred sexuality. By engaging in breathwork, meditation, sacred touch, and energy exchange, individuals and partners can deepen their connection to the divine feminine and facilitate spiritual awakening. The integration of these practices into daily life can lead to enhanced intimacy, healing, and personal empowerment.

Part IV: Walking the Path of the Divine Feminine

The Dark Night of the Soul – Transformation Through Suffering and Surrender

The concept of the "Dark Night of the Soul" is a profound spiritual experience that signifies a deep and transformative period of suffering, introspection, and eventual awakening. Originating from the mystical writings of **Saint John of the Cross** in the 16th century, the term describes a state where an individual feels lost, disconnected, and engulfed by darkness. This experience can often lead to profound personal transformation, spiritual growth, and a renewed sense of purpose. In this discussion, we will explore the characteristics, causes, and transformative potential of the Dark Night of the Soul, as well as how to navigate this challenging experience.

---

1. Understanding the Dark Night of the Soul

A. Definition and Origins

The Dark Night of the Soul refers to a spiritual crisis marked by feelings of abandonment, despair, and a sense of disconnection from the divine. It often follows a period of intense spiritual awakening or growth, during which an individual may confront their deepest fears, insecurities, and attachments. This term was popularized by Saint John of the Cross in his poem and commentary "The Dark Night," which describes the soul's journey through darkness toward union with God.

B. Stages of the Dark Night

The Dark Night typically unfolds in stages:

1. **Awakening:** The individual begins to experience a heightened sense of awareness and spiritual insight, often marked by a desire for deeper connection with the divine.
2. **Crisis:** The initial enthusiasm fades, leading to feelings of disillusionment, confusion, and emotional turmoil. The individual may feel abandoned by the divine and question their beliefs.
3. **Surrender:** The individual reaches a point of surrender, letting go of attachments, expectations, and the need for control. This stage often involves a willingness to confront and embrace suffering.
4. **Transformation:** Through surrender, the individual begins to integrate their experiences, gaining insights and wisdom. This stage may lead to a renewed sense of purpose, clarity, and connection with the divine.

---

2. Characteristics of the Dark Night of the Soul

For our free video kundalini training visit https://shiftnetwork.infusionsoft.com/go/akeg/a20331

A. Emotional and Psychological Symptoms

Individuals experiencing the Dark Night may encounter various emotional and psychological symptoms, including:

- **Feelings of Isolation:** A sense of disconnection from others, community, and even the divine.
- **Depression and Anxiety:** Intense feelings of despair, hopelessness, or anxiety may arise as the individual grapples with their inner turmoil.
- **Loss of Identity:** A crisis of identity occurs as long-held beliefs, values, and attachments are challenged and dismantled.
- **Existential Questions:** Individuals may grapple with profound questions about the meaning of life, purpose, and existence.

B. Spiritual Symptoms

In addition to emotional symptoms, individuals may also experience spiritual challenges, such as:

- **Loss of Faith:** Doubts about one's beliefs or connection to the divine may surface, leading to feelings of abandonment or confusion.
- **Darkness and Despair:** An overwhelming sense of darkness, emptiness, or despair that may feel all-encompassing.
- **Increased Sensitivity:** Heightened sensitivity to energies, emotions, and environments, leading to feelings of overwhelm.

---

3. Causes of the Dark Night of the Soul

A. Spiritual Awakening

Often, the Dark Night is triggered by a significant spiritual awakening or transformative experience. As individuals begin to expand their consciousness and connect with deeper truths, they may encounter aspects of themselves that they have long suppressed or ignored.

B. Life Transitions and Crises

Major life transitions, such as loss, trauma, relationship changes, or health crises, can act as catalysts for the Dark Night. These experiences force individuals to confront their vulnerabilities and question their beliefs and values.

C. The Journey of Healing

For those on a healing journey, unresolved trauma, emotional pain, or deep-seated fears may surface, prompting a Dark Night experience. The process of healing often requires navigating the depths of suffering to achieve transformation.

4. Navigating the Dark Night of the Soul

A. Embracing Surrender

Surrender is a crucial aspect of navigating the Dark Night. This involves letting go of control, accepting the present moment, and trusting the process. Embracing surrender allows individuals to move through their suffering without resistance, facilitating healing and transformation.

B. Practicing Self-Compassion

Cultivating self-compassion is essential during this challenging period. Acknowledging and accepting one's pain, rather than judging or denying it, creates space for healing. Gentle self-care practices, such as mindfulness, journaling, and meditation, can foster self-compassion.

C. Seeking Support

Connecting with trusted friends, spiritual mentors, or therapists can provide valuable support during the Dark Night. Sharing one's experiences and feelings can alleviate isolation and create a sense of community.

D. Engaging in Spiritual Practices

Incorporating spiritual practices, such as meditation, prayer, yoga, or journaling, can help individuals connect with their inner selves and the divine. These practices provide grounding and insight, facilitating the journey through darkness.

E. Reflecting on Insights and Lessons

As individuals navigate the Dark Night, it's essential to reflect on the insights and lessons that arise. Journaling about experiences, emotions, and revelations can foster greater self-awareness and understanding.

5. The Transformative Potential of the Dark Night

A. Personal Growth and Transformation

The Dark Night of the Soul can lead to profound personal growth and transformation. By confronting fears, limitations, and attachments, individuals emerge with a deeper understanding of themselves and their connection to the divine.

B. Strengthened Spiritual Connection

Navigating the darkness often leads to a more authentic and profound spiritual connection. Individuals may develop a more nuanced understanding of their faith and beliefs, ultimately enhancing their spiritual journey.

C. Integration and Wholeness

The process of surrender and healing allows individuals to integrate all aspects of themselves, including their shadows. This integration fosters a sense of wholeness, self-acceptance, and authenticity.

The Dark Night of the Soul is a challenging yet transformative experience that can lead to profound personal and spiritual growth. By embracing suffering and surrendering to the process, individuals can navigate this darkness and emerge with a deeper understanding of themselves and their connection to the divine. While the journey may be difficult, it ultimately offers the potential for renewal, clarity, and a more authentic life.

Shakti and the Moon Cycles – Tapping into Lunar Energy for Spiritual Growth

The moon has long been regarded as a powerful symbol of feminine energy, intuition, and emotional depth. In many spiritual traditions, including Hinduism, the moon is associated with **Shakti**, the divine feminine energy that embodies creation, nurturing, and transformation. Understanding the relationship between Shakti and the moon cycles allows individuals to harness lunar energy for personal and spiritual growth. This discussion will explore the significance of the moon in Shakti practices, the phases of the moon, and how to utilize lunar energy for empowerment and transformation.

---

1. The Symbolism of the Moon in Spirituality

A. The Moon as a Feminine Archetype

The moon is often seen as a representation of the divine feminine, embodying qualities such as intuition, receptivity, and emotional fluidity. Unlike the sun, which represents active, masculine energy, the moon reflects the softer, nurturing aspects of Shakti. Many cultures and spiritual traditions view the moon as a guiding force for women's cycles, fertility, and spiritual growth.

B. The Relationship Between Shakti and Lunar Energy

Shakti, as the primal energy of creation, is deeply interconnected with the cycles of the moon. Just as the moon goes through phases, so too does Shakti manifest in various forms throughout the cycles of life. Tapping into lunar energy allows individuals to align with Shakti's dynamic qualities and access deeper levels of awareness and intuition.

2. The Phases of the Moon and Their Energetic Significance

The moon goes through eight primary phases, each with its own unique energy and significance. Understanding these phases allows individuals to harness the specific qualities of Shakti that align with their spiritual intentions.

A. New Moon (Amavasya)

- **Energy:** The new moon represents new beginnings, intention setting, and the seed of potential. It is a time for introspection and reflection.
- **Shakti Practices:** Engage in meditation and journaling to set intentions for the lunar cycle. Create a vision board or perform a ritual to honor new beginnings.

B. Waxing Crescent Moon

- **Energy:** As the moon begins to grow, this phase symbolizes growth, expansion, and the manifestation of intentions.
- **Shakti Practices:** Focus on nurturing the intentions set during the new moon. Practice affirmations and take small steps toward your goals. This is a good time for creative pursuits.

C. First Quarter Moon

- **Energy:** The first quarter moon signifies determination, action, and overcoming challenges. It is a time of decision-making and commitment.
- **Shakti Practices:** Engage in activities that require focus and willpower. Reflect on any obstacles that may arise and how to overcome them. Consider performing a physical practice, such as yoga or dance, to channel your energy.

D. Waxing Gibbous Moon

- **Energy:** This phase is about refinement, evaluation, and preparation for culmination. It encourages assessment of progress and fine-tuning of intentions.
- **Shakti Practices:** Review your goals and intentions, making any necessary adjustments. Engage in practices that promote gratitude and appreciation for your journey so far.

E. Full Moon (Purnima)

- **Energy:** The full moon represents peak energy, abundance, and illumination. It is a time of celebration, completion, and release.
- **Shakti Practices:** Participate in rituals to celebrate achievements and express gratitude. This is also an excellent time for releasing what no longer serves you, whether through journaling or ritualistic burning of intentions.

F. Waning Gibbous Moon

- **Energy:** This phase signifies reflection, introspection, and release. It is a time to evaluate experiences and let go of attachments.
- **Shakti Practices:** Reflect on the lessons learned during the full moon. Engage in cleansing practices, such as salt baths or sage smudging, to clear out stagnant energy.

G. Last Quarter Moon

- **Energy:** The last quarter moon is associated with closure, forgiveness, and introspection. It encourages individuals to let go of what is no longer needed.
- **Shakti Practices:** Perform rituals for forgiveness and closure. Journal about what you wish to release, both emotionally and physically.

H. Waning Crescent Moon

- **Energy:** This phase symbolizes rest, renewal, and contemplation. It is a time to recharge and prepare for the new moon cycle.
- **Shakti Practices:** Engage in restorative practices, such as meditation, yoga, or spending time in nature. Focus on self-care and nurturing your inner self in preparation for the new cycle.

---

3. Practical Ways to Tap into Lunar Energy for Spiritual Growth

A. Lunar Rituals and Ceremonies

Creating and participating in rituals during specific moon phases can enhance your connection to Shakti and lunar energy. Consider performing ceremonies that include:

- **Lighting Candles:** Use candles to symbolize intentions during the new moon and full moon. The light represents clarity and manifestation.
- **Creating Moon Water:** Collect water during the full moon, allowing it to absorb lunar energy. Use it in rituals, blessings, or to enhance your spiritual practices.

B. Meditation and Visualization

Meditation is a powerful tool for connecting with lunar energy. During moon phases, practice visualizations that align with the energy of that phase. For example:

- **New Moon Visualization:** Visualize planting seeds of intention in fertile soil, allowing your desires to grow.
- **Full Moon Meditation:** Visualize yourself surrounded by the radiant light of the full moon, feeling illuminated and abundant.

C. Journaling and Reflection

Keep a lunar journal to track your intentions, insights, and experiences during each moon phase. This practice can help you recognize patterns in your emotional and spiritual growth over time. Reflect on how lunar energy influences your life, emotions, and spiritual journey.

D. Connect with Nature

Spend time in nature during significant moon phases. Observe how the moon affects the tides, plant life, and wildlife. Connecting with the natural world enhances your understanding of Shakti and the cyclical nature of life.

E. Movement and Dance

Incorporate dance or movement practices that honor the lunar cycles. Each moon phase can inspire different styles of movement. For example:

- **Full Moon Dance:** Engage in expressive dance to celebrate abundance and joy.
- **New Moon Flow:** Practice slow, grounding movements that encourage introspection and intention-setting.

---

4. The Benefits of Tapping into Lunar Energy

A. Increased Intuition and Awareness

Aligning with the lunar cycles fosters heightened intuition and self-awareness. Individuals become more attuned to their inner guidance and emotional states.

B. Enhanced Emotional Regulation

Understanding the energy of each moon phase allows individuals to navigate their emotions more effectively. By working with lunar energy, one can learn to release negativity and embrace positive growth.

C. Empowerment and Manifestation

Harnessing lunar energy for intention-setting and manifestation can lead to greater empowerment. Individuals can take an active role in shaping their lives and aligning with their true purpose.

D. Deepened Spiritual Connection

Tapping into lunar energy facilitates a deeper connection with the divine and the feminine aspects of Shakti. This connection can lead to transformative experiences and personal growth.

The relationship between Shakti and the moon cycles offers a profound opportunity for spiritual growth and transformation. By understanding and embracing the energies of the lunar phases, individuals can tap into their own divine feminine essence, nurture their intentions, and cultivate deeper connections with themselves and the universe. Engaging in lunar practices empowers individuals to navigate their spiritual journey with clarity, purpose, and grace.

The Warrior Goddess Archetype – Channeling Inner Strength Through Kali Energy

The Warrior Goddess archetype embodies the fierce, protective, and transformative aspects of the divine feminine. Central to this archetype is **Kali**, the Hindu goddess of destruction and regeneration, who represents the primal energy of creation and the fierce protector against negativity and fear. This discussion will explore the characteristics of the Warrior Goddess archetype, the significance of Kali in spiritual practices, and how to channel her energy for empowerment and transformation.

1. Understanding the Warrior Goddess Archetype

A. Definition and Characteristics

The Warrior Goddess archetype embodies strength, courage, resilience, and the ability to confront adversity. This archetype transcends gender and can be accessed by anyone seeking to tap into their inner power. Key characteristics include:

- **Fearlessness:** The Warrior Goddess faces challenges with courage and conviction, unafraid to stand up for what is right.

- **Protectiveness:** She embodies a protective nature, safeguarding not only herself but also others, particularly those who are vulnerable or marginalized.

- **Transformational Power:** The Warrior Goddess symbolizes transformation, embracing change as a means to growth and renewal.

- **Intuition and Instinct:** She relies on her intuition and instincts, guiding her decisions and actions in alignment with her true self.

B. Kali as the Embodiment of the Warrior Goddess

Kali, one of the most revered forms of the divine feminine in Hinduism, epitomizes the Warrior Goddess archetype. Known as the goddess of time, change, and destruction, Kali's energy is fierce yet nurturing, helping her devotees navigate the complexities of life. She is often depicted with dark skin, a fierce expression, and adorned with a necklace of skulls, symbolizing the destruction of ego and the liberation of the soul.

2. The Significance of Kali in Spiritual Practices

A. Kali's Role in Hindu Mythology

In Hindu mythology, Kali emerged during a battle between the gods and demons when the goddess Durga needed assistance. Kali manifested from Durga's brow to annihilate the demon Raktabija, who could replicate himself from each drop of blood. Kali's ferocity in battle illustrates the importance of confronting negativity and chaos in the world.

B. Kali as a Symbol of Transformation

Kali represents the cycle of death and rebirth. Her destructive nature is not meant to instill fear but rather to facilitate transformation and liberation. By breaking down outdated beliefs and attachments, Kali clears the path for new beginnings, embodying the Warrior Goddess's role in personal and spiritual growth.

C. Kali in Tantric Practices

In Tantric practices, Kali is revered as a powerful force of transformation and liberation. Her energy is invoked to awaken Kundalini, the primal life force that resides at the base of the spine. Practitioners channel Kali's fierce energy to overcome obstacles, release fears, and embrace their true selves.

---

3. Channeling Kali Energy for Empowerment

A. Cultivating Inner Strength

Channeling Kali energy involves tapping into one's inner strength and resilience. Here are practical ways to embody this energy:

- **Meditation and Visualization:** Engage in meditation focused on Kali, visualizing her fierce presence. Imagine drawing her energy into your being, empowering you to confront challenges with confidence.
- **Affirmations:** Use affirmations that embody Kali's strength and determination. Phrases such as "I am powerful" or "I embrace transformation" can help reinforce this energy in your life.

B. Embracing the Shadow Self

Kali teaches the importance of embracing the shadow self—the parts of ourselves that we may hide or deny. To channel her energy, individuals can:

- **Self-Reflection:** Engage in journaling or introspection to confront fears, insecurities, and limiting beliefs. Acknowledge these aspects as part of your journey toward wholeness.

- **Shadow Work:** Participate in shadow work practices, such as guided meditations or therapy, to integrate and heal unresolved emotions.

C. Practicing Fierce Compassion

The Warrior Goddess embodies fierce compassion, standing up for oneself and others. To channel this energy:

- **Advocacy:** Become an advocate for yourself and those in need. Stand up for justice, equality, and empowerment, embodying Kali's protective nature.
- **Self-Care:** Prioritize self-care and self-love, recognizing that nurturing yourself is essential for maintaining strength and resilience.

D. Rituals and Offerings

Creating rituals to honor Kali can enhance your connection to her energy. Consider:

- **Altar Creation:** Set up an altar dedicated to Kali, adorned with images, candles, and offerings of flowers or fruits. Spend time in contemplation and prayer at this sacred space.
- **Ceremonial Practices:** Participate in rituals that invoke Kali's energy, such as fire ceremonies, where you can symbolically release negativity and invite transformation.

---

4. The Benefits of Channeling Kali Energy

A. Empowerment and Confidence

Tapping into Kali's fierce energy empowers individuals to take bold actions, confront fears, and pursue their desires with confidence.

B. Enhanced Resilience

Embracing the Warrior Goddess archetype fosters resilience, allowing individuals to navigate life's challenges with strength and grace.

C. Spiritual Transformation

Channeling Kali energy facilitates spiritual transformation, guiding individuals toward greater self-awareness, healing, and liberation from limiting beliefs.

D. Connection to the Divine Feminine

Engaging with Kali deepens the connection to the divine feminine, allowing individuals to honor and embody their inner strength and intuition.

The Warrior Goddess archetype, embodied by Kali, serves as a powerful source of strength, courage, and transformation. By channeling her energy, individuals can confront challenges, embrace their inner power, and navigate the complexities of life with confidence and resilience. Embracing the Warrior Goddess within not only fosters personal empowerment but also promotes a deeper connection to the divine feminine and the transformative energy of Shakti.

Shakti in Relationships – Divine Union and Conscious Partnerships

The concept of **Shakti** extends beyond individual spiritual development and into the realm of relationships. In the context of partnerships, Shakti embodies the divine feminine energy that fosters connection, creativity, and growth. This discussion will explore how Shakti influences relationships, the importance of conscious partnerships, and ways to cultivate divine union through mutual empowerment and understanding.

1. Understanding Shakti in Relationships

A. The Essence of Shakti

Shakti, often associated with the divine feminine, represents the creative and dynamic force that underlies all life. In relationships, Shakti symbolizes the energy of connection, intimacy, and transformation. This energy encourages both partners to express their true selves, supporting a partnership that is both nurturing and empowering.

B. The Balance of Masculine and Feminine Energies

Healthy relationships often require a balance of masculine and feminine energies, where Shakti (the feminine) complements **Shiva** (the masculine). Shiva represents stability, presence, and consciousness, while Shakti embodies creativity, intuition, and emotion. In a conscious partnership, both energies work harmoniously, creating a foundation for growth and understanding.

2. The Importance of Conscious Partnerships

A. Defining Conscious Partnerships

Conscious partnerships are relationships built on awareness, mutual respect, and intentionality. These partnerships prioritize open communication, emotional intimacy, and shared growth. In a conscious partnership, both individuals are committed to understanding themselves and each other on a deeper level.

B. Characteristics of Conscious Partnerships

Key features of conscious partnerships include:

For our free video kundalini training visit https://shiftnetwork.infusionsoft.com/go/akeg/a20331

- **Mutual Empowerment:** Partners uplift and inspire each other, encouraging personal and spiritual growth.
- **Open Communication:** Honest and transparent communication is a cornerstone of the relationship, allowing for vulnerability and emotional sharing.
- **Emotional Intelligence:** Both partners develop emotional awareness, enabling them to navigate challenges and conflicts with compassion.
- **Shared Vision:** A shared vision for the future aligns the partners' goals and aspirations, creating a sense of unity.

---

3. Cultivating Divine Union Through Shakti

A. Embracing Vulnerability

Vulnerability is essential in fostering a deep connection. Embracing vulnerability allows partners to express their authentic selves, fostering intimacy and trust. To cultivate vulnerability:

- **Share Feelings:** Create a safe space for open dialogue about emotions, fears, and desires. Encourage each other to express feelings without judgment.
- **Active Listening:** Practice active listening, showing empathy and understanding when your partner shares their experiences. This strengthens emotional bonds.

B. Practicing Presence and Mindfulness

Mindfulness in relationships enhances awareness and connection. Being present with each other cultivates deeper intimacy. Techniques include:

- **Mindful Communication:** Approach conversations with full attention and presence. Avoid distractions and practice active engagement.
- **Shared Mindfulness Practices:** Engage in mindfulness practices together, such as meditation or yoga, to enhance your connection to each other and the divine.

C. Nurturing Creativity and Passion

Shakti embodies creativity and passion, which can enhance relationships. To nurture these qualities:

- **Engage in Creative Activities:** Explore shared hobbies or creative pursuits, such as art, dance, or music, that allow both partners to express their individuality while bonding together.
- **Cultivate Passion:** Make time for romance and intimacy. Prioritize date nights, surprise gestures, and open discussions about desires and fantasies.

D. Supporting Each Other's Spiritual Growth

In a conscious partnership, both individuals support each other's spiritual journeys. This can be achieved by:

- **Encouraging Self-Discovery:** Promote self-exploration and personal development, allowing each partner to flourish as an individual.
- **Shared Spiritual Practices:** Participate in spiritual practices together, such as meditation, rituals, or attending workshops, to deepen your connection to each other and the divine.

---

4. The Role of Conflict and Resolution in Relationships

A. Understanding Conflict as a Catalyst for Growth

Conflict is a natural part of any relationship, but it can also serve as an opportunity for growth and transformation. Embracing conflict with a Shakti mindset involves viewing challenges as chances to deepen understanding and connection.

B. Approaching Conflict with Compassion

When conflicts arise, approach them with compassion and empathy:

- **Stay Grounded:** Maintain emotional awareness and composure during disagreements. Practice self-regulation techniques to avoid escalating tensions.
- **Focus on Solutions:** Shift the focus from blame to collaboration. Work together to find solutions that honor both partners' needs.

C. Forgiveness and Letting Go

Forgiveness is essential for healing and moving forward. To cultivate forgiveness:

- **Acknowledge Hurt:** Validate each other's feelings and experiences. Acknowledge the impact of actions on both partners.
- **Let Go of Resentment:** Practice letting go of past grievances to create space for healing and renewal in the relationship.

---

5. The Transformative Power of Shakti in Relationships

A. Creating a Sacred Space for Love

Shakti energy transforms relationships by creating a sacred space for love and connection. This space encourages both partners to be their authentic selves, fostering trust and intimacy.

B. Embracing Change and Growth

As partners evolve, so do their needs and desires. Embracing change and supporting each other through transitions allows for a deeper understanding of the relationship's dynamic.

C. Celebrating the Journey Together

Recognizing the journey as a partnership deepens the connection. Celebrate milestones, both big and small, and acknowledge the growth you've experienced together.

Shakti plays a vital role in fostering divine union and conscious partnerships. By embracing vulnerability, practicing mindfulness, nurturing creativity, and supporting each other's spiritual growth, partners can cultivate a deeper connection grounded in mutual respect and understanding. The transformative power of Shakti in relationships creates a sacred space for love, intimacy, and growth, ultimately leading to a harmonious union that embodies the divine feminine and masculine energies.

Shakti and Creativity – How Kundalini Fuels Artistic and Inspired Expression

The relationship between **Shakti**, the divine feminine energy, and creativity is profound and transformative. Shakti represents the primal force of creation, manifesting in all forms of artistic and inspired expression. When awakened, **Kundalini** energy, often depicted as a coiled serpent at the base of the spine, rises through the chakras, unlocking creative potential and allowing individuals to tap into their inner artist. This discussion explores the connection between Shakti and creativity, the role of Kundalini in artistic expression, and ways to harness this energy for creative endeavors.

---

1. Understanding Shakti and Its Creative Energy

A. The Essence of Shakti

Shakti is the embodiment of dynamic energy and creativity in the universe. It is the life force that drives creation, innovation, and inspiration. As the divine feminine, Shakti nurtures and supports the flow of creativity, allowing individuals to express their unique visions and ideas.

B. The Role of Creativity in Spiritual Expression

Creativity is an essential aspect of spiritual expression, allowing individuals to connect with their inner selves and the divine. Artistic endeavors serve as a medium for exploring emotions, thoughts, and experiences, facilitating self-discovery and spiritual growth.

2. The Kundalini Energy and Its Influence on Creativity

A. Kundalini Awakening and Creative Flow

The awakening of Kundalini energy initiates a process of transformation that can significantly impact creative expression. As Kundalini rises through the chakras, it activates various aspects of the self, including:

- **Enhanced Intuition:** The rise of Kundalini heightens intuition, allowing individuals to tap into their inner wisdom and creative insights. This intuitive awareness can guide artistic endeavors and inspire innovative ideas.
- **Emotional Release:** The movement of Kundalini through the energy centers can lead to the release of pent-up emotions, resulting in a cathartic experience that fuels creative expression. Artists often channel these emotions into their work, creating powerful and resonant art.
- **Heightened Sensitivity:** Kundalini awakening increases sensitivity to the world, allowing individuals to perceive beauty, inspiration, and meaning in their surroundings. This heightened awareness can lead to a deeper connection with the creative process.

B. The Chakras and Their Creative Influence

Each chakra corresponds to different aspects of creativity and expression:

1. **Root Chakra (Muladhara):** Grounding energy that provides a foundation for creative expression. A balanced root chakra fosters stability and security, allowing for the exploration of creativity.
2. **Sacral Chakra (Svadhisthana):** The center of emotions, desires, and sexuality. This chakra fuels passion and the creative impulse, making it essential for artistic expression.
3. **Solar Plexus Chakra (Manipura):** Associated with personal power and confidence. A strong solar plexus chakra empowers individuals to express their creativity boldly.
4. **Heart Chakra (Anahata):** The center of love and compassion. Creativity flows from a heart-centered place, allowing for genuine expression and connection with others.
5. **Throat Chakra (Vishuddha):** The center of communication and self-expression. This chakra is vital for articulating creative ideas and sharing artistic work with the world.
6. **Third Eye Chakra (Ajna):** The center of intuition and insight. A balanced third eye enhances creative vision and the ability to manifest ideas into reality.

7. **Crown Chakra (Sahasrara):** The connection to the divine and universal consciousness. Creativity that arises from this chakra is often inspired and transcendent, linking the artist to higher realms of thought.

---

3. Nurturing Creativity Through Shakti and Kundalini

A. Practices for Awakening Kundalini

To harness the creative potential of Shakti and Kundalini, individuals can engage in various practices:

1. **Meditation:** Regular meditation can help awaken Kundalini and deepen self-awareness. Focus on the breath and visualize energy rising through the chakras to facilitate the flow of creativity.
2. **Yoga:** Kundalini yoga is a powerful practice that combines movement, breathwork, and meditation to awaken Kundalini energy. Specific postures, or asanas, are designed to activate the chakras and promote creative expression.
3. **Pranayama (Breath Control):** Breathwork techniques help regulate energy flow within the body. Practices such as **Kapalabhati** (breath of fire) and **Nadi Shodhana** (alternate nostril breathing) can stimulate the Kundalini energy and enhance creative flow.
4. **Creative Rituals:** Engage in rituals that honor the creative process. This can include lighting candles, setting intentions for artistic projects, and creating a sacred space for inspiration.

B. Embracing Playfulness and Experimentation

Creativity thrives in an environment of playfulness and experimentation. To nurture this aspect:

- **Explore Different Mediums:** Try various forms of artistic expression, such as painting, writing, dancing, or music. Allow yourself to experiment without the pressure of perfection.
- **Practice Spontaneity:** Engage in spontaneous creative activities, allowing intuition to guide your choices. Embrace the freedom to create without limitations.

C. Connecting with Nature

Nature is a powerful source of inspiration and a manifestation of Shakti. Spend time in natural settings to reconnect with the creative energy of the earth. Observe the beauty around you, allowing it to fuel your artistic expression.

4. The Transformative Power of Creativity

A. Healing Through Creative Expression

Engaging in creative activities can be a healing process, allowing individuals to express and release emotions, traumas, and experiences. This therapeutic aspect of creativity aligns with the transformative nature of Shakti and Kundalini.

B. Building Community and Connection

Sharing creative work fosters community and connection with others. By expressing oneself authentically, individuals can inspire others and create a sense of belonging. This aligns with Shakti's nurturing aspect, as creativity connects people on a deeper level.

C. Empowerment Through Artistic Expression

Harnessing Shakti and Kundalini for creative expression empowers individuals to reclaim their voices and assert their identities. Art becomes a vehicle for self-discovery and empowerment, reflecting the unique perspectives and experiences of the artist.

The connection between Shakti and creativity is a powerful force that can fuel artistic and inspired expression. By awakening Kundalini energy and nurturing the creative process, individuals can tap into their inner artist, embracing the transformative power of Shakti. Through practices such as meditation, yoga, and playful experimentation, one can cultivate a deeper connection to their creativity and express their unique voice. Embracing this divine energy not only enhances personal artistic endeavors but also fosters a sense of community and connection with others, celebrating the beauty of human expression.

Shakti in Nature – The Earth's Kundalini and Sacred Power Spots

The concept of **Shakti** transcends human experience, resonating deeply within the natural world. In many spiritual traditions, the Earth itself is viewed as a living entity imbued with Shakti, the divine feminine energy that nourishes and sustains all life. This discussion will explore the idea of the Earth's Kundalini, its manifestation in nature, and the significance of sacred power spots around the globe.

---

1. Understanding Shakti in Nature

A. The Essence of Shakti

Shakti is often described as the primordial energy that underlies creation, creativity, and transformation. It is dynamic, nurturing, and sustaining, manifesting in various forms throughout the natural world. In nature, Shakti is experienced as the life force that animates plants, animals, and ecosystems.

B. The Concept of Earth's Kundalini

The idea of the Earth's Kundalini refers to a latent energy that resides within the planet, similar to the Kundalini energy within humans. This energy is believed to be coiled at specific points on Earth, analogous to the coiled serpent at the base of the spine in individuals. When activated, this energy can rise through the Earth's energy centers, or chakras, facilitating spiritual awakening and transformation.

---

2. The Earth's Energy Centers (Chakras)

A. Sacred Sites as Energy Centers

Many cultures and spiritual traditions recognize specific locations on Earth as sacred power spots, often associated with the Earth's energy centers. These locations are believed to be conduits of Shakti, where the energy is amplified and accessible for spiritual practices, healing, and transformation. Some notable sacred sites include:

1. **Mount Shasta (California, USA):** Considered one of the root chakras of the Earth, Mount Shasta is believed to be a powerful energy vortex, attracting spiritual seekers and healers. Its natural beauty and vibrant energy offer a deep connection to Shakti.

2. **Sedona (Arizona, USA):** Known for its stunning red rock formations, Sedona is renowned for its vortexes that are said to enhance spiritual energy. Many people visit Sedona for healing, meditation, and creative inspiration.

3. **Glastonbury (England):** Often associated with the legendary Isle of Avalon, Glastonbury is believed to be a heart chakra of the Earth. The Tor, a prominent hill, serves as a powerful focal point for spiritual practices and connections to the divine feminine.

4. **Uluru (Ayers Rock, Australia):** A sacred site for the Indigenous peoples of Australia, Uluru is considered a major energy center and a symbol of the Earth's sacredness. Its presence invokes a sense of connection to the land and its ancestral spirits.

5. **The Pyramids of Giza (Egypt):** These ancient structures are believed to be aligned with cosmic energy and serve as powerful conduits of Shakti. Many practitioners visit the pyramids for meditation, healing, and spiritual awakening.

B. Energetic Lines and Ley Lines

In addition to specific power spots, the Earth is crisscrossed by energetic pathways known as **ley lines**. These lines are thought to connect various sacred sites, facilitating the flow of Shakti across the planet. Ley lines are believed to carry the Earth's energy, making them significant for those seeking spiritual alignment and connection.

3. Experiencing Shakti in Nature

A. Nature as a Source of Inspiration

Nature is a powerful expression of Shakti, offering opportunities for connection, healing, and creativity. Engaging with the natural world allows individuals to experience the divine feminine energy in its purest form. Ways to connect with Shakti in nature include:

1. **Nature Walks and Hikes:** Spend time in natural settings to immerse yourself in the beauty and tranquility of the environment. Observing the cycles of nature can inspire feelings of interconnectedness and appreciation.
2. **Mindful Observation:** Practice mindfulness in nature by paying attention to the sights, sounds, and sensations around you. Allow yourself to be fully present in the moment, connecting with the life force of the Earth.
3. **Rituals and Offerings:** Create rituals to honor the Earth and its sacred energy. This can include making offerings of flowers, herbs, or other natural materials as a way to express gratitude and reverence.

B. Healing Through Nature

Nature provides a healing environment that can rejuvenate the body, mind, and spirit. Exposure to natural landscapes, plants, and water can reduce stress, enhance well-being, and promote spiritual growth. Practices such as **forest bathing** (Shinrin-yoku) and eco-therapy utilize nature's healing qualities to support mental and emotional health.

4. The Interconnection of Shakti and the Earth

A. The Cycle of Life and Death

Shakti embodies the cycle of life, death, and rebirth, which is evident in the natural world. The processes of growth, decay, and renewal in nature reflect the transformative power of Shakti. Understanding this cycle can deepen one's appreciation for life and foster a sense of reverence for the Earth.

B. The Role of Indigenous Wisdom

Many Indigenous cultures recognize the sacredness of the Earth and its energy. Their traditions often include teachings about living in harmony with nature, honoring the land, and understanding the interconnectedness of all living beings. This wisdom emphasizes the importance of maintaining a respectful relationship with the Earth and acknowledging its Shakti.

The presence of Shakti in nature is a profound reminder of the interconnectedness of all life. By recognizing the Earth as a living entity imbued with divine feminine energy, individuals can cultivate a deeper connection to the planet and its sacred power spots. Engaging with nature, exploring sacred sites, and honoring the cycles of life can enhance spiritual growth and foster a sense of unity with the world around us. Embracing Shakti in nature not only enriches personal spiritual practice but also nurtures a deeper understanding of our place within the larger web of existence.

Part V: Embodying the Divine Feminine

Living as an Embodied Goddess – Integrating Shakti into Daily Life

Living as an embodied goddess involves embracing the energy of **Shakti** in all aspects of life. Shakti represents the divine feminine power that resides within each individual, empowering them to express their true selves and embody creativity, compassion, and strength. Integrating Shakti into daily life allows individuals to connect with their inner goddess, cultivating a deeper sense of purpose, fulfillment, and harmony. This discussion will explore practical ways to embody Shakti in everyday life, including mindset shifts, rituals, and practices that honor the divine feminine.

---

1. Understanding the Embodied Goddess

A. The Essence of the Embodied Goddess

The embodied goddess is a representation of the divine feminine energy that exists within all beings, transcending gender. This concept encompasses qualities such as intuition, creativity, nurturing, empowerment, and sensuality. To live as an embodied goddess is to recognize and celebrate these qualities in oneself, allowing for authentic self-expression and connection to the divine.

B. Shakti as a Source of Power

Shakti, the divine feminine force, is the source of creativity, transformation, and life itself. When individuals tap into Shakti, they harness the power to create, heal, and inspire. This energy fosters resilience and empowers individuals to navigate challenges with grace and strength.

---

2. Cultivating the Mindset of an Embodied Goddess

A. Embrace Self-Love and Acceptance

Living as an embodied goddess begins with cultivating self-love and acceptance. This involves recognizing one's inherent worth and embracing imperfections. Practices to foster self-love include:

- **Affirmations:** Use positive affirmations to reinforce self-worth and cultivate a loving relationship with oneself. For example, "I am a powerful expression of Shakti" or "I honor my body and my unique gifts."

- **Self-Care Rituals:** Prioritize self-care by engaging in activities that nourish the body, mind, and spirit. This may include taking baths, enjoying nature, practicing yoga, or spending time in creative pursuits.

B. Connect with Intuition and Inner Wisdom

The embodied goddess trusts her intuition and inner guidance. Cultivating this connection involves:

- **Meditation and Reflection:** Regular meditation allows individuals to quiet the mind and access deeper insights. Use guided meditations focused on connecting with the divine feminine or Shakti.
- **Journaling:** Maintain a journal to explore thoughts, emotions, and intuitive insights. Writing can help clarify feelings and strengthen the connection to inner wisdom.

3. Daily Rituals to Honor Shakti

A. Morning Rituals

Start each day with rituals that honor Shakti and set a positive tone:

- **Gratitude Practice:** Upon waking, express gratitude for the day ahead. This can be done through silent reflection or by writing in a gratitude journal.
- **Sacred Movement:** Engage in morning movement practices such as yoga, dance, or stretching. This helps awaken the body and connect with Shakti's energy.

B. Rituals Throughout the Day

Integrate rituals into daily routines to maintain a connection to Shakti:

- **Mindful Eating:** Approach meals as sacred moments, savoring each bite and expressing gratitude for the nourishment. This practice fosters a sense of connection to the body and the Earth.
- **Nature Connection:** Spend time outdoors, whether through walks in nature, gardening, or simply observing the natural world. This helps to ground oneself and honor the life force present in all living things.

C. Evening Rituals

Close the day with rituals that promote reflection and gratitude:

- **Candle Lighting:** Light a candle in the evening as a symbol of honoring the divine feminine. Use this time to meditate, journal, or set intentions for the next day.
- **Release and Let Go:** Practice a releasing ritual, where you let go of any negativity or stress from the day. This can involve writing down what you wish to release and safely burning the paper.

4. Nurturing Relationships with the Divine Feminine

A. Cultivating Sisterhood and Community

Engage with other women and individuals who embody the divine feminine. Building connections with like-minded souls fosters empowerment and support. Consider:

- **Women's Circles:** Join or create a women's circle where participants can share experiences, celebrate each other's successes, and support personal growth.
- **Collaboration:** Collaborate with others on creative projects, workshops, or spiritual practices that celebrate the divine feminine.

B. Honoring the Feminine in Relationships

Integrate Shakti into personal relationships by nurturing emotional connection and communication. This involves:

- **Open Dialogue:** Encourage honest and open conversations with partners, friends, and family. Share feelings, aspirations, and fears to deepen understanding and intimacy.
- **Celebrating Femininity:** Create rituals or celebrations that honor the feminine aspects of relationships, such as sharing stories of empowerment or celebrating milestones together.

---

5. Expressing Creativity as an Embodied Goddess

A. Channeling Shakti into Creative Expression

Engaging in creative activities allows individuals to express their unique gifts and connect with Shakti. Explore various forms of artistic expression:

- **Art and Craft:** Experiment with painting, drawing, pottery, or any other form of visual art. Allow the creative process to flow naturally, free from judgment.
- **Dance and Movement:** Use dance as a way to connect with Shakti. Whether through free movement or structured dance forms, allow your body to express emotions and creativity.

B. Writing and Storytelling

Writing can be a powerful medium for self-expression and exploration of the divine feminine. Consider:

- **Poetry and Prose:** Write poetry, short stories, or personal reflections that honor your journey as an embodied goddess. Explore themes of empowerment, creativity, and connection.

- **Storytelling:** Share personal stories or the stories of women who inspire you. This can be done through spoken word events, workshops, or written publications.

6. Living in Alignment with Nature

A. Nature as a Teacher

Recognize the lessons and wisdom found in nature. Living in alignment with the cycles of nature fosters a deeper connection to Shakti:

- **Seasonal Practices:** Align personal practices with the changing seasons. For example, during spring, focus on renewal and growth, while autumn can be a time for reflection and letting go.
- **Earth-Based Rituals:** Create rituals that honor the elements (earth, water, fire, air) and their connection to the divine feminine. This can involve creating altars, offering gratitude, or engaging in ceremonies that celebrate nature.

Living as an embodied goddess means embracing the divine feminine energy of Shakti in every aspect of life. By cultivating self-love, connecting with intuition, engaging in daily rituals, nurturing relationships, expressing creativity, and aligning with nature, individuals can embody the qualities of the goddess. This journey of integration fosters empowerment, self-discovery, and a deeper connection to the sacred energy that resides within and around us. Embracing the essence of Shakti allows for a fulfilling and vibrant life, where each moment becomes an opportunity for creativity, love, and connection to the divine.

Healing the Wounded Feminine – Overcoming Generational Trauma and Repression

The concept of the **Wounded Feminine** refers to the collective pain and trauma experienced by women throughout history, often stemming from patriarchal systems, societal repression, and cultural narratives that diminish feminine power. Healing this wounded aspect is crucial for individual and collective transformation, allowing individuals to reclaim their feminine energy, strength, and authenticity. This discussion delves into the roots of generational trauma, the impact of repression, and practical approaches to healing the wounded feminine.

1. Understanding the Wounded Feminine

A. The Nature of the Wounded Feminine

The Wounded Feminine represents the aspects of femininity that have been suppressed, marginalized, or distorted due to historical and societal influences. This can manifest as feelings of unworthiness, disconnection from one's body, self-doubt, and internalized misogyny.

B. Generational Trauma

Generational trauma refers to the transmission of trauma across generations, often affecting how individuals relate to themselves and others. This trauma can be linked to:

- **Cultural Narratives:** Societal beliefs that devalue femininity, promote competition among women, and enforce rigid gender roles contribute to the wounded feminine.
- **Family Dynamics:** Patterns of behavior and emotional responses learned from mothers, grandmothers, and other female figures can perpetuate feelings of inadequacy, fear, and disempowerment.
- **Historical Oppression:** The legacy of oppression faced by women, including violence, discrimination, and societal exclusion, creates a collective wound that can be felt across generations.

---

2. Recognizing the Impact of Repression

A. Psychological and Emotional Effects

The repression of feminine energy can lead to a variety of psychological and emotional issues, including:

- **Low Self-Esteem:** The internalization of societal messages that diminish feminine value can result in a lack of confidence and self-worth.
- **Disconnection from Body:** Repression may cause individuals to dissociate from their bodies, leading to issues such as body image concerns, eating disorders, and physical ailments.
- **Fear of Expression:** A fear of being judged or rejected may hinder self-expression, creativity, and authentic communication.

B. Interpersonal Relationships

The wounded feminine can also impact relationships with others:

- **Codependency:** The need for external validation and approval can lead to codependent relationships, where individuals rely on others for self-worth.
- **Competition vs. Collaboration:** The wounded feminine may foster competition among women, creating barriers to sisterhood, support, and collective empowerment.

- **Difficulty with Boundaries:** Struggles with asserting boundaries can stem from a lack of self-respect and fear of conflict, leading to unhealthy relationship dynamics.

3. Healing the Wounded Feminine

Healing the wounded feminine is a multifaceted process that involves personal, communal, and spiritual approaches. Here are several key strategies for facilitating this healing:

A. Acknowledgment and Awareness

The first step in healing is acknowledging the existence of the wounded feminine and its impact:

- **Reflect on Family History:** Engage in conversations with family members to understand the historical narratives and experiences that have shaped your lineage. This may include exploring the stories of female ancestors and their struggles.
- **Journaling:** Write about personal experiences related to the wounded feminine, including feelings of inadequacy, trauma, and repression. This practice fosters awareness and provides a safe space for emotional expression.

B. Reclaiming the Body

Connecting with the body is essential for healing the wounded feminine:

- **Body Positivity Practices:** Engage in practices that celebrate and honor your body, such as body-positive affirmations, mirror work, or movement that feels joyful and liberating.
- **Embodied Movement:** Practices like yoga, dance, and other forms of physical expression can help individuals reconnect with their bodies and release stored trauma. Mindful movement encourages individuals to listen to their bodies and honor their needs.

C. Cultivating Self-Compassion

Developing self-compassion is vital for healing:

- **Practice Forgiveness:** Release self-blame and judgment by practicing forgiveness towards yourself and others. Recognize that healing is a journey and that it's okay to have setbacks.
- **Nurture Inner Dialogue:** Replace negative self-talk with compassionate and affirming statements. Treat yourself with the kindness you would offer to a friend.

D. Sisterhood and Community

Building supportive relationships with other women fosters healing:

- **Join Women's Circles:** Participate in women's circles or support groups that focus on sharing experiences, healing, and empowerment. These gatherings create safe spaces for vulnerability and connection.
- **Collaborative Projects:** Engage in collaborative creative projects with other women, such as art, writing, or community initiatives. Working together can strengthen bonds and promote a sense of shared purpose.

E. Spiritual Practices

Integrate spiritual practices that honor the feminine:

- **Rituals and Ceremonies:** Create personal rituals that honor the feminine, such as moon ceremonies, honoring the cycles of nature, or celebrating feminine deities that resonate with you.
- **Meditation and Visualization:** Use meditation techniques to connect with the divine feminine. Visualizations can include inviting healing energy into your life or envisioning yourself as a strong, empowered goddess.

---

4. Overcoming Cultural and Societal Barriers

A. Challenging Societal Norms

Healing the wounded feminine involves challenging societal norms that perpetuate oppression and disempowerment:

- **Advocacy and Activism:** Engage in advocacy for gender equality, women's rights, and social justice. Supporting movements that uplift women can contribute to collective healing.
- **Educating Others:** Share knowledge about the wounded feminine and the importance of healing within communities. Raising awareness can empower others to address their own wounds and support collective healing.

B. Redefining Femininity

Redefining the narrative around femininity is essential for healing:

- **Embrace Diverse Expressions of Femininity:** Celebrate the diversity of feminine expression by recognizing that femininity can take many forms, including strength, independence, creativity, and nurturing qualities.
- **Challenge Stereotypes:** Confront stereotypes that diminish feminine power, and actively promote representations of strong, empowered women in media, literature, and everyday life.

Healing the wounded feminine is a transformative journey that requires acknowledgment, compassion, and collective effort. By addressing generational trauma, overcoming repression, and embracing practices that honor the divine feminine, individuals can reclaim their power and authenticity. This healing journey not only benefits individuals but also contributes to the collective empowerment of women and the healing of societal wounds. As we embrace our inner goddesses, we create a world where feminine energy is celebrated, respected, and integrated into every aspect of life, fostering harmony, creativity, and balance.

The Rise of the Feminine in the Modern Age – Shakti's Role in the Global Awakening

The rise of the feminine in the modern age represents a significant shift in societal values, perspectives, and power dynamics. As women and feminine energy gain visibility and empowerment, a collective awakening occurs that challenges patriarchal norms and embraces the qualities of the Divine Feminine, or **Shakti**. This discussion explores the role of Shakti in the global awakening, highlighting how the resurgence of feminine energy influences various aspects of life, including spirituality, social justice, creativity, and personal empowerment.

1. Understanding Shakti in the Context of Modern Awakening

A. The Essence of Shakti

Shakti, in Hindu philosophy, represents the creative and dynamic energy of the Divine Feminine. It embodies qualities such as intuition, nurturing, compassion, strength, and resilience. In the context of modern awakening, Shakti symbolizes a resurgence of feminine power and wisdom, calling for balance between masculine and feminine energies within individuals and society.

B. The Global Context of the Awakening

The modern age is characterized by significant shifts in gender dynamics, cultural values, and spiritual understanding. The rise of the feminine reflects a broader movement towards:

- **Gender Equality:** Advocacy for women's rights, representation, and empowerment is gaining momentum globally, challenging systemic inequalities and patriarchal structures.
- **Spiritual Reclamation:** Many individuals are returning to spiritual practices that honor the feminine, reclaiming traditions that have historically been marginalized or suppressed.

- **Holistic Approaches:** The recognition of holistic healing, emotional intelligence, and community-oriented approaches is increasing, aligning with the nurturing aspects of Shakti.

2. The Feminine Awakening in Society

A. Social Justice and Activism

The rise of the feminine is closely tied to movements advocating for social justice and equality:

- **Women's Movements:** The #MeToo movement, gender pay equity campaigns, and reproductive rights activism are examples of women asserting their rights and demanding systemic change. These movements emphasize the need to honor women's voices and experiences.
- **Intersectionality:** Modern feminism embraces intersectionality, recognizing that issues of race, class, sexuality, and ability intersect with gender. This holistic approach empowers marginalized voices and fosters inclusive dialogues.

B. Redefining Leadership and Power

The awakening of the feminine challenges traditional notions of leadership and power:

- **Collaborative Leadership:** Feminine leadership emphasizes collaboration, empathy, and inclusivity rather than dominance and competition. This shift encourages leaders to create environments where diverse voices are heard and valued.
- **Emotional Intelligence:** The importance of emotional intelligence in leadership and workplace dynamics reflects feminine qualities that prioritize relational understanding, communication, and conflict resolution.

3. Spiritual Reclamation and Shakti

A. Reconnecting with Spiritual Traditions

As the feminine rises, there is a growing interest in reclaiming spiritual traditions that honor the Divine Feminine:

- **Goddess Worship:** Many individuals are exploring and honoring goddess archetypes from various cultures, recognizing the wisdom and strength embodied by figures such as Kali, Lakshmi, and the Virgin Mary. This reclamation fosters a deeper connection to feminine energy and empowerment.
- **Tantric Practices:** Tantric traditions, which emphasize the sacredness of the body and the divine union of masculine and feminine energies, are gaining

popularity. These practices encourage individuals to explore their sexuality, sensuality, and creative potential as expressions of Shakti.

B. Inner Awakening and Personal Empowerment

The rise of the feminine encourages personal healing and empowerment:

- **Healing the Wounded Feminine:** Many individuals are engaging in practices that address generational trauma, self-acceptance, and body positivity. This healing journey empowers individuals to embrace their authentic selves and reclaim their feminine energy.
- **Creative Expression:** The awakening of the feminine inspires individuals to channel their creativity through art, writing, music, and other forms of self-expression. Shakti is seen as the driving force behind inspiration and artistic endeavors.

---

4. The Role of Shakti in Global Consciousness

A. Shakti and Environmental Awareness

The rise of the feminine is also reflected in increased environmental consciousness and sustainability efforts:

- **Ecofeminism:** This movement connects feminism with ecological concerns, advocating for the protection of the Earth and promoting sustainable practices. Ecofeminism emphasizes the interconnectedness of all living beings and the importance of nurturing the planet as a reflection of feminine energy.
- **Holistic Healing Practices:** The resurgence of holistic and natural healing practices, such as herbalism, yoga, and mindfulness, aligns with the nurturing qualities of Shakti. These practices encourage individuals to connect with nature and honor the Earth's rhythms.

B. Global Sisterhood and Solidarity

The rise of the feminine fosters a sense of global sisterhood and solidarity among women:

- **Support Networks:** Women are forming networks and communities that provide support, mentorship, and collaboration. These connections create safe spaces for sharing experiences and empowering one another.
- **Cultural Exchange:** The sharing of diverse cultural practices and wisdom strengthens the collective understanding of the feminine. Women from different backgrounds are coming together to celebrate their unique expressions of femininity and advocate for common causes.

5. Challenges and Opportunities in the Awakening

A. Navigating Resistance

While the rise of the feminine presents opportunities for growth and transformation, it also faces challenges:

- **Patriarchal Resistance:** Efforts to reclaim feminine power may encounter resistance from patriarchal structures that seek to maintain the status quo. This can manifest as backlash against feminist movements, attempts to silence women's voices, and cultural stigmatization.
- **Internalized Oppression:** Women may struggle with internalized beliefs and self-doubt stemming from historical oppression, leading to challenges in fully embracing their feminine power and asserting their voices.

B. Embracing Transformation

Despite challenges, the awakening of the feminine offers opportunities for transformation:

- **Collective Empowerment:** As more individuals embrace the qualities of Shakti and engage in healing practices, a collective shift occurs that fosters empowerment and resilience.
- **Holistic Healing:** The integration of holistic healing modalities promotes emotional and spiritual well-being, enabling individuals to navigate challenges with grace and strength.

The rise of the feminine in the modern age signifies a powerful transformation in societal values, relationships, and individual empowerment. Shakti plays a crucial role in this awakening, guiding individuals to reconnect with their inner strength, creativity, and authenticity. As the Divine Feminine rises, it fosters a collective consciousness that values compassion, collaboration, and holistic understanding.

This awakening is not only a reclaiming of feminine power but also a call for balance, unity, and healing in a world often dominated by fear and division. By embracing Shakti and nurturing the feminine within ourselves and our communities, we contribute to a more just, compassionate, and harmonious world.

Balancing Shakti and Shiva Within – The Sacred Dance of Masculine and Feminine Energies

For our free video kundalini training visit https://shiftnetwork.infusionsoft.com/go/akeg/a20331

The interplay between **Shakti** and **Shiva** embodies the dynamic relationship between the feminine and masculine energies present in all individuals. In Hindu philosophy, Shakti represents the creative, nurturing, and transformative aspects of the Divine Feminine, while Shiva symbolizes the protective, stabilizing, and conscious aspects of the Divine Masculine. Balancing these energies within ourselves is essential for holistic well-being, spiritual growth, and a harmonious life. This discussion explores the significance of Shakti and Shiva, their characteristics, and practical approaches to achieving balance.

---

1. Understanding Shakti and Shiva

A. The Nature of Shakti

- **Divine Feminine Energy:** Shakti is the primordial energy that fuels creation, transformation, and sustenance. It encompasses qualities such as intuition, emotion, receptivity, and nurturing.
- **Dynamic Power:** Shakti is often depicted as the creative force behind all manifestations in the universe, driving change and evolution. It can be fierce, as seen in goddesses like Kali, or nurturing, like Lakshmi.
- **Emotional Intelligence:** Shakti embodies emotional depth, compassion, and the ability to connect with oneself and others on a profound level.

B. The Nature of Shiva

- **Divine Masculine Energy:** Shiva represents the consciousness, stillness, and awareness that provides the foundation for creation. He embodies qualities such as strength, protection, discipline, and transcendence.
- **Transcendent Awareness:** Shiva is often associated with the formless, eternal aspect of existence, symbolizing the importance of stillness and presence in the midst of chaos.
- **Inner Guidance:** Shiva represents the inner guidance and wisdom that allows individuals to navigate life's challenges with clarity and purpose.

---

2. The Interplay of Shakti and Shiva

A. Complementary Energies

- **Mutual Support:** Shakti and Shiva are not opposing forces but complementary energies that support and enhance each other. Shakti needs the structure and awareness of Shiva to manifest her creative potential, while Shiva requires the dynamism and vitality of Shakti to bring his vision into form.

- **Sacred Union:** The union of Shakti and Shiva represents the harmonious integration of masculine and feminine energies, leading to spiritual wholeness and enlightenment. This balance allows individuals to experience life fully, embracing both their nurturing and assertive qualities.

B. The Sacred Dance

- **Dance of Creation:** The relationship between Shakti and Shiva can be viewed as a sacred dance, where both energies flow together in a rhythm of creation, transformation, and dissolution. This dance symbolizes the cycles of life, death, and rebirth, reflecting the interconnectedness of all things.
- **Cyclic Nature:** The dance of Shakti and Shiva can be seen in natural cycles such as the changing seasons, lunar phases, and the ebb and flow of life experiences. Recognizing these cycles helps individuals attune themselves to the balance of energies within.

---

3. Importance of Balancing Shakti and Shiva

A. Personal Empowerment

- **Embracing Wholeness:** Balancing Shakti and Shiva allows individuals to embrace their full spectrum of capabilities. This integration fosters self-acceptance, confidence, and a sense of completeness.
- **Authentic Expression:** When both energies are in balance, individuals can express themselves authentically, utilizing their creative potential (Shakti) while remaining grounded and focused (Shiva).

B. Enhanced Relationships

- **Healthy Dynamics:** A balanced integration of Shakti and Shiva promotes healthy dynamics in relationships. Partners can support each other's growth while maintaining their individuality, leading to more fulfilling and harmonious connections.
- **Collaboration:** The recognition of both energies encourages collaboration and mutual respect, enabling individuals to celebrate each other's strengths without competition or conflict.

C. Spiritual Growth

- **Holistic Development:** Balancing Shakti and Shiva supports holistic spiritual development, allowing individuals to access deeper states of consciousness and awareness.

- **Integration of Experience:** The dance between these energies facilitates the integration of life experiences, enabling individuals to learn from challenges and cultivate wisdom through both nurturing and strength.

---

4. Practical Approaches to Balancing Shakti and Shiva

A. Self-Reflection and Awareness

- **Inner Dialogue:** Engage in self-reflection to explore your inner landscape. Identify which energies dominate your life and how they influence your thoughts, emotions, and behaviors.
- **Journaling:** Maintain a journal to record your thoughts, feelings, and experiences related to both Shakti and Shiva. Reflect on situations where you feel more aligned with one energy over the other and consider how to integrate the missing aspects.

B. Practices for Cultivating Shakti

- **Creative Expression:** Engage in artistic pursuits, such as painting, dancing, or writing, to channel Shakti's creative energy. Allow yourself to express emotions freely and explore your imaginative potential.
- **Nurturing Rituals:** Create rituals that honor your body and emotions. This could include self-care practices, such as baths, meditation, or time spent in nature, allowing you to connect with your nurturing side.

C. Practices for Cultivating Shiva

- **Meditation and Stillness:** Incorporate meditation practices that promote stillness and awareness. Focus on breathwork or mindfulness techniques to cultivate inner peace and presence.
- **Discipline and Structure:** Set boundaries and establish routines that help create stability and focus in your life. This discipline fosters the clarity and direction associated with Shiva.

D. Integrative Practices

- **Yoga and Movement:** Engage in yoga practices that honor both energies. Flowing styles (like Vinyasa) can cultivate Shakti, while grounding practices (like Hatha) can connect you to Shiva. Explore poses that encourage balance, such as tree pose or warrior pose.
- **Sacred Dance:** Participate in dance practices that allow for spontaneous movement. This encourages the free flow of energy while grounding yourself in the present moment.

5. Challenges in Balancing Shakti and Shiva

A. Societal Pressures

- **Cultural Conditioning:** Societal norms often reinforce rigid definitions of masculinity and femininity, leading individuals to suppress one energy in favor of the other. Challenging these stereotypes requires conscious effort and self-awareness.
- **Fear of Vulnerability:** Embracing Shakti may involve confronting fears around vulnerability, emotional expression, and intuition. Societal expectations can create resistance to fully embracing these qualities.

B. Internal Conflicts

- **Shadow Work:** Balancing these energies may bring unresolved emotional wounds to the surface. Engaging in shadow work—acknowledging and integrating suppressed emotions and experiences—can facilitate healing and growth.
- **Duality of Existence:** Navigating the duality of existence can be challenging. Individuals may struggle with the interplay between strength and vulnerability, action and receptivity, leading to feelings of confusion or imbalance.

Balancing Shakti and Shiva within ourselves is a lifelong journey that requires self-awareness, compassion, and commitment. By recognizing and honoring the interplay between these energies, individuals can experience profound personal growth, spiritual development, and healthier relationships.

Embracing the sacred dance of Shakti and Shiva encourages a holistic understanding of oneself, fostering authenticity and wholeness. As we integrate these energies, we contribute to a more balanced and harmonious world where both feminine and masculine qualities are celebrated and revered.

The Shakti Sisterhood – Collective Healing and the Rise of the Divine Feminine Community

The concept of the **Shakti Sisterhood** embodies a collective movement among women and feminine-identifying individuals to embrace their inner power, share their experiences, and support one another in healing and growth. This sisterhood represents a reawakening of the Divine Feminine, fostering a community where individuals can come together to celebrate their unique expressions of Shakti—the creative and transformative energy within. This discussion explores the significance of the Shakti Sisterhood, its roots in collective healing, and its role in the modern spiritual landscape.

1. Understanding the Shakti Sisterhood

A. Definition of Shakti Sisterhood

The Shakti Sisterhood refers to a supportive community of women and those who resonate with the feminine energy, coming together to honor, nurture, and empower one another. It emphasizes the importance of sisterhood, connection, and collaboration, recognizing that collective healing can lead to personal and societal transformation.

B. The Essence of Shakti

- **Creative Energy:** Shakti is the embodiment of the Divine Feminine, representing the life force that drives creativity, intuition, and emotional depth. It is often associated with goddesses like Durga, Kali, and Lakshmi, who exemplify different aspects of feminine power.
- **Empowerment and Healing:** Embracing Shakti involves recognizing and reclaiming the power within oneself. The Shakti Sisterhood serves as a platform for women to explore their identities, share their stories, and heal from past traumas collectively.

2. Historical Context of the Shakti Sisterhood

A. Ancient Traditions

- **Women's Gatherings:** Throughout history, women have gathered in sacred circles to share wisdom, support one another, and engage in rituals that honor the Divine Feminine. These gatherings were often spaces for healing, creativity, and spiritual growth.
- **Goddess Worship:** Many ancient cultures revered goddesses as symbols of feminine power and wisdom. The resurgence of interest in these archetypes today informs the principles of the Shakti Sisterhood, promoting the idea that women can reclaim their power through the lens of the Divine Feminine.

B. Modern Feminist Movements

- **Second Wave Feminism:** The feminist movements of the 20th century paved the way for women to assert their rights and challenge patriarchal structures. These movements emphasized sisterhood, solidarity, and collective action.
- **Spiritual Feminism:** The rise of spiritual feminism in the late 20th century encouraged women to reconnect with their spiritual roots and embrace the

Divine Feminine. This movement laid the groundwork for the Shakti Sisterhood, blending feminist principles with spiritual exploration.

3. Collective Healing and the Shakti Sisterhood

A. Shared Experiences

- **Creating Safe Spaces:** The Shakti Sisterhood fosters environments where women can share their stories, struggles, and triumphs without judgment. These safe spaces promote vulnerability and authenticity, allowing for deeper connections.
- **Empathy and Understanding:** Through sharing experiences, members of the sisterhood cultivate empathy and understanding. This collective sharing serves as a powerful healing tool, helping individuals feel seen, heard, and validated.

B. Healing Practices

- **Rituals and Ceremonies:** The Shakti Sisterhood often incorporates rituals and ceremonies that honor feminine energy, such as full moon gatherings, goddess worship, and intention-setting circles. These practices facilitate connection with the Divine Feminine and promote healing on both personal and collective levels.
- **Workshops and Retreats:** Many sisterhoods offer workshops and retreats focused on personal development, emotional healing, and spiritual growth. These gatherings provide opportunities for participants to learn new skills, explore their creativity, and connect with like-minded individuals.

C. Addressing Wounded Feminine Energy

- **Healing Generational Trauma:** The Shakti Sisterhood plays a crucial role in addressing and healing generational trauma related to the repression of feminine energy. By sharing stories and engaging in healing practices, members work to break cycles of trauma and reclaim their power.
- **Empowerment through Connection:** Collective healing fosters a sense of empowerment among participants, encouraging them to embrace their individuality while recognizing their interconnectedness with other women.

4. The Rise of the Divine Feminine Community

A. Expanding the Sisterhood

- **Inclusivity and Diversity:** The Shakti Sisterhood embraces inclusivity, welcoming individuals from diverse backgrounds, cultures, and experiences.

This diversity enriches the community and broadens perspectives on the Divine Feminine.

- **Intersectionality:** Recognizing that the experiences of women are influenced by factors such as race, class, sexuality, and ability, the Shakti Sisterhood fosters discussions around intersectionality. This allows for a more nuanced understanding of the challenges faced by different individuals.

B. Global Movement

- **Online Communities:** The rise of digital platforms has enabled the Shakti Sisterhood to expand beyond geographical boundaries. Online communities provide spaces for women to connect, share resources, and support each other regardless of location.
- **Social Media Activism:** Many members use social media to raise awareness about issues affecting women, promote healing practices, and celebrate the Divine Feminine. This activism strengthens the sense of community and collective purpose.

C. Spiritual Awakening

- **Reconnecting with Spirituality:** The Shakti Sisterhood encourages members to reconnect with their spiritual roots and explore practices that honor the Divine Feminine. This spiritual awakening fosters a deeper understanding of oneself and the world.
- **Collective Consciousness:** As more individuals embrace the principles of the Shakti Sisterhood, a collective consciousness emerges that values compassion, empathy, and collaboration. This shift contributes to a more harmonious and balanced world.

---

5. Practical Steps to Engage with the Shakti Sisterhood

A. Forming Sisterhood Circles

- **Gathering Together:** Women can create local sisterhood circles to foster community and support. These circles can meet regularly to share experiences, engage in rituals, and discuss topics related to feminine empowerment.
- **Creating Safe Spaces:** Establish guidelines for open communication and confidentiality, ensuring that all participants feel safe to express themselves and share their stories.

B. Engaging in Healing Practices

- **Rituals and Ceremonies:** Incorporate rituals that honor the Divine Feminine, such as moon ceremonies, goddess invocations, and intention-setting practices.

These rituals help participants connect with their inner power and celebrate their uniqueness.

- **Workshops and Events:** Organize workshops focused on personal development, creative expression, and spiritual growth. Invite guest speakers, facilitators, or healers to share their knowledge and expertise.

C. Online Engagement

- **Social Media Connections:** Join online platforms, forums, and groups dedicated to the Divine Feminine and women's empowerment. Engage in discussions, share resources, and support one another in the digital space.
- **Virtual Events:** Participate in online workshops, webinars, and retreats that focus on healing, empowerment, and collective growth. This allows for broader participation and connection.

---

6. Challenges and Opportunities within the Shakti Sisterhood

A. Challenges

- **Resistance to Vulnerability:** Some individuals may struggle with opening up and being vulnerable in a group setting, stemming from past trauma or societal conditioning.
- **Cultural Differences:** Navigating cultural differences within the sisterhood may present challenges, as individuals may have varying beliefs and practices related to femininity and spirituality.

B. Opportunities

- **Deepening Connections:** The challenges faced can ultimately lead to deeper connections and understanding among members, fostering growth and resilience.
- **Collective Empowerment:** As members navigate challenges together, they cultivate a sense of collective empowerment, reinforcing the idea that healing is a shared journey.

The Shakti Sisterhood represents a powerful movement toward collective healing, empowerment, and the celebration of the Divine Feminine. By coming together in community, women and feminine-identifying individuals can reclaim their inner power, support one another in healing, and foster a sense of belonging.

As the Shakti Sisterhood continues to grow and evolve, it embodies the principles of compassion, inclusivity, and collaboration, contributing to a global awakening of the feminine spirit. By honoring and nurturing the energy of Shakti, members of the sisterhood create a ripple effect that extends beyond themselves, influencing families, communities, and the world.

The Ultimate Liberation: Moksha and Shakti's Final Gift – The Journey to Enlightenment

The concept of **Moksha**—the ultimate liberation or spiritual freedom—is central to various Indian philosophies, particularly within Hinduism. It represents the soul's release from the cycle of birth, death, and rebirth (samsara), achieving a state of eternal bliss and unity with the Divine. In this context, **Shakti**, the Divine Feminine energy, plays a pivotal role in guiding individuals toward this ultimate state of enlightenment. This discussion explores the relationship between Moksha and Shakti, the significance of this journey, and the transformative practices that facilitate the attainment of enlightenment.

1. Understanding Moksha

A. Definition of Moksha

- **Spiritual Liberation:** Moksha is defined as the liberation of the soul from the cycle of samsara. It is the realization of one's true nature as the eternal self (Atman), free from the constraints of material existence.
- **Unity with the Divine:** Achieving Moksha means attaining oneness with Brahman (the universal consciousness or ultimate reality), leading to a state of eternal peace, joy, and fulfillment.

B. Paths to Moksha

- **Jnana Yoga (Path of Knowledge):** This path emphasizes self-inquiry and the pursuit of knowledge to discern the difference between the transient world and eternal reality.
- **Bhakti Yoga (Path of Devotion):** Bhakti involves devotion to a personal deity, fostering love and surrender as a means to attain union with the Divine.
- **Karma Yoga (Path of Selfless Action):** This path focuses on performing selfless actions without attachment to the fruits of those actions, purifying the heart and mind.
- **Raja Yoga (Path of Meditation):** Raja Yoga involves disciplined practices of meditation and physical postures (asanas) to attain control over the mind and body, facilitating spiritual awakening.

2. The Role of Shakti in the Journey to Moksha

A. Shakti as the Divine Feminine Energy

- **Creative and Transformative Force:** Shakti represents the dynamic energy of creation, transformation, and spiritual evolution. She embodies the nurturing, intuitive, and compassionate aspects of the Divine Feminine, guiding individuals on their spiritual journey.
- **Catalyst for Awakening:** Shakti serves as a catalyst for spiritual awakening, empowering individuals to transcend their limitations and realize their true nature. This empowerment is essential for progressing toward Moksha.

B. Shakti and the Kundalini Energy

- **Kundalini Awakening:** Kundalini is often associated with Shakti as the coiled energy residing at the base of the spine. The awakening of Kundalini involves the rising of this energy through the chakras, leading to heightened states of consciousness and spiritual insight.
- **Pathway to Enlightenment:** As Kundalini rises and integrates with Shakti, it facilitates a profound transformation of the individual. This process can lead to moments of enlightenment and ultimately prepare the seeker for the experience of Moksha.

---

3. The Journey to Enlightenment

A. Spiritual Evolution and Self-Realization

- **Self-Discovery:** The journey to Moksha involves deep self-inquiry and exploration of one's identity beyond societal conditioning. This process requires individuals to confront their fears, desires, and attachments, ultimately leading to self-realization.
- **Ego Dissolution:** The dissolution of the ego—a sense of separate self—is crucial for experiencing Moksha. Shakti assists in this process by challenging limiting beliefs and guiding individuals toward a deeper understanding of their true essence.

B. The Role of Spiritual Practices

- **Meditation and Mindfulness:** Regular meditation practices cultivate awareness, presence, and inner stillness. These practices allow individuals to connect with Shakti and facilitate the rise of Kundalini energy.
- **Devotional Practices:** Engaging in devotional practices, such as chanting mantras, participating in rituals, or connecting with the Divine Feminine through

goddess worship, deepens the bond with Shakti and fosters a sense of surrender and love.

- **Selfless Service (Seva):** Practicing selfless service cultivates humility, compassion, and detachment from personal gain. This aligns the practitioner with the flow of Shakti and purifies the heart, moving them closer to Moksha.

4. The Final Gift of Shakti: Attaining Moksha

A. The Experience of Moksha

- **Unity with the Divine:** Upon achieving Moksha, the individual experiences a profound sense of unity with the Divine, transcending the illusion of separation. This state is characterized by bliss, love, and an understanding of the interconnectedness of all beings.
- **Liberation from Suffering:** Moksha represents the end of all suffering, desires, and attachments, allowing the soul to rest in its true nature. This liberation brings lasting peace and fulfillment.

B. Shakti's Blessing

- **Empowerment and Grace:** Shakti's final gift is the empowerment to recognize and embrace one's true nature. This grace enables individuals to navigate the challenges of life with courage and wisdom, ultimately leading them to liberation.
- **Continuity of Energy:** Even after achieving Moksha, the energy of Shakti continues to flow through the enlightened being, contributing to the upliftment and healing of others. Enlightened individuals often become beacons of light and inspiration, guiding others on their paths to awakening.

5. The Challenges on the Path to Moksha

A. Overcoming Obstacles

- **Inner Resistance:** Individuals may face inner resistance to change, stemming from fear, attachments, or unresolved traumas. Shakti helps individuals confront these barriers and transform them into opportunities for growth.
- **Societal Expectations:** Cultural and societal conditioning can create obstacles on the spiritual path. Embracing Shakti encourages individuals to break free from these constraints and forge their own paths toward enlightenment.

B. Maintaining Balance

- **Integration of Shakti and Shiva:** Achieving Moksha requires a balance between Shakti (feminine energy) and Shiva (masculine energy). This balance supports the holistic development of the individual and facilitates a smoother transition to enlightenment.

The journey to **Moksha** is a profound spiritual quest that involves the awakening of **Shakti** and the realization of one's true nature. Through self-inquiry, devotion, and the practice of spiritual disciplines, individuals can cultivate the qualities necessary for enlightenment.

Shakti serves as a guiding force, empowering seekers to transcend their limitations and embrace their inner divinity. The final gift of Shakti is the realization of unity with the Divine and liberation from the cycle of birth and death.

Printed in Great Britain
by Amazon